Music

Nicholas Cook is Professor
of Music and Dean of Arts at the
University of Southampton; he has
also taught in Hong Kong, Australia
and the USA. His publications
include *A Guide to Musical Analysis*
(1987), *Music, Imagination, and
Culture* (1990), *Beethoven: Symphony
No. 9* (1993), *Analysis Through
Composition* (1996), and *Analysing
Musical Multimedia* (1998).

A VERY SHORT INTRODUCTION

Very Short Introductions offer stimulating, accessible introductions to a wide variety of subjects, demonstrating the finest contemporary thinking about their central problems and issues.

Other Very Short Introductions available from Oxford Paperbacks:

Archaeology
Paul Bahn

Buddhism
Damien Keown

Classics
Mary Beard and John Henderson

Hinduism
Kim Knott

Islam
Malise Ruthven

Judaism
Norman Solomon

Literary Theory
Jonathan Culler

Music
Nicholas Cook

Politics
Kenneth Minogue

Psychology
Gillian Butler and Freda
    McManus

Forthcoming from Oxford Paperbacks:

The Bible
John Riches

Economics
Partha Dasgupta

The Koran
Michael Cook

Law
Stephen Guest and Jeffrey Jowell

Social and Cultural Anthropology
John Monaghan and Peter Just

Sociology
Steve Bruce

Theology
David Ford

Music

A VERY SHORT INTRODUCTION

Nicholas Cook

Oxford   New York
OXFORD UNIVERSITY PRESS
1998

Oxford University Press, Great Clarendon Street, Oxford OX2 6DP

Oxford New York

Athens Auckland Bangkok Bogota Bombay Buenos Aires
Calcutta Cape Town Dar es Salaam Delhi Florence Hong Kong Istanbul
Karachi Kuala Lumpur Madras Madrid Melbourne Mexico City
Nairobi Paris Singapore Taipei Tokyo Toronto Warsaw

and associated companies in
Berlin Ibadan

Oxford is a trade mark of Oxford University Press

British Library Cataloguing in Publication Data
Data available

Library of Congress Cataloging in Publication Data
Data available

ISBN 0–19–285340-6 (Pbk.)

10 9 8 7 6 5 4 3 2 1

Typeset by Best-set Typesetter Ltd., Hong Kong
Printed in Great Britain by
Mackays of Chatham PLC
Chatham, Kent

Foreword

On 31 August 1997 the finals of the Mercury Music Prize were televised. The nominations included Suede, Mark Anthony Turnage, the Chemical Brothers, and John Tavener. And what is so remarkable about that? Just that only a few years earlier it would have been unusual for 'classical' composers like Turnage and Tavener to appear on the same stage as pop groups like Suede and the Chemical Brothers, and inconceivable for them to be judged against one another. (The winners, though, were Roni Size and the Reprazent Collective, well known in the Bristol jungle scene.) But then, it was just a week later that Tavener's 'Song for Athene' featured alongside Elton (now Sir Elton) John's rendition of 'Candle in the Wind' at Princess Diana's funeral. And the following month (Sir) Paul McCartney's choral and orchestral composition *Standing Stone* received its première in London's Royal Albert Hall. Meanwhile, on the other side of the Atlantic, doctoral students are already writing dissertations on the work of Frank Zappa, which ranged from acid rock to classical concert music. Everywhere the barriers that once kept different styles and traditions of music firmly apart are crumbling.

It's an obvious fact that the world is teeming with different kinds of music: traditional, folk, classical, jazz, rock, pop, world, just to name a few. This has always been the case, but modern communications and sound reproduction technology have made musical pluralism part of everyday life. (You can *hear* this every time you walk through a shopping mall.) And yet the ways we think about music don't reflect this. Each type of music comes with its own way of thinking about music, as if it were the only way of thinking about music (and the only music to think about). In particular, the way of thinking about music that is built into schools and universities—

and most books about music, for that matter—reflects the way music was in nineteenth-century Europe rather than the way it is today, anywhere. The result is a kind of credibility gap between music and how we think about it.

In this *Very Short Introduction* I want to put all music on the map. Or rather, given that it is a *very* short introduction, I want to spread out a map that all music could in principle be put on to, if only there were space for it. And this has a clear knock-on effect in terms of what this book *isn't*. What it isn't is an ABC of music, providing a potted summary of the so-called rudiments (staves, clefs, scales, chords, and the rest) followed by a quick romp through the repertory. The reason it can't be an ABC of music is that it would have to be not just an ABC but an ΑΒΓ, an АБГ, and an נבא, not to mention an あ い う. If you can sensibly talk about music having an alphabet at all, then every music has its own alphabet. Seen that way, every music would need its own *Very Short Introduction*.

Every music is different, but every music is music, too. There is a level at which you can talk of 'music' (and I can write this *Very Short Introduction*), but it isn't the ABC level. To talk about music in general is to talk about what music means—and more basically, how it is (how it can be) that music operates as an agent of meaning. For music isn't just something nice to listen to. On the contrary, it's deeply embedded in human culture (just as there isn't a culture that doesn't have language, so there isn't one that doesn't have music). Music somehow seems to be natural, to exist as something apart—and yet it is suffused with human values, with our sense of what is good or bad, right or wrong. Music doesn't just happen, it is what we make it, and what we make *of* it. People *think* through music, decide who they are through it, express themselves through it.

So this book is as much about thinking about music as it is about music. And it is also about the social and institutional structures that condition thinking about music. The book begins with an individual, domestic response to music—with a television commercial, and the different associations and connotations that give it meaning—and ends with a snapshot of how people are thinking, and writing, about music in today's academic world. (As George Miller, my editor at Oxford University Press, put it, it is at this point that a gang of musicologists turn up and take over.) In focusing the final chapter on issues of music and gender, I don't want to give the impression that musicologists have sex on the brain. But there has long been an academic tradition of thinking of music as 'purely musical', as being about nothing but itself, which has created a general impression among everyone *except* musicologists that in that case music can't matter very much. More than anything, it is the study of music and gender that has put music's worldly meaning back on the musico-logical map and so led musicology, in a word, out of the closet.

And of course, music *does* matter; if I didn't believe it, I wouldn't have written this book, and if you didn't believe it, you wouldn't be reading this sentence. Rather than being something apart, music is in the very midst of things. In fact it is less a 'something' than a way of knowing the world, a way of being ourselves—though, as I shall explain in Chapter 4, the metaphor of music being a kind of object is built deep into its history. You might almost say that music isn't a 'something' until, by thinking and writing about it, we turn it into one. If that sounds a bit paradoxical, the reason is that it *is* a bit paradoxical; maybe Elvis Costello (if it was Elvis Costello) had a point when he said that writing about music is like dancing about architecture. But the point is that we do it all the same. We use words to say what music cannot say, to say what we *mean* by music, what music means to us. And in the end, it is largely words that determine what music *does* mean to us. That is perhaps the only real justification for writing anything about music, even a *Very Short Introduction*.

But short as it is, a book with as broad a scope as this

exceeds the bounds of any individual's expertise; at least, it exceeds the bounds of mine. Whatever mistakes may remain, my thanks to Mark Everist, Matthew Head, Roger Parker, Robynn Stilwell, and Jonathan Stock, without whom there would have been more of them.

N.C.

Contents

List of Illustrations

1 Musical Values

A Television Commercial

'I want to be . . . *a musician*.' Those are the opening words in a television commercial for Prudential pension plans which was being broadcast in late 1992. It begins with a young man sitting back in a chair, a dreamy, wistful expression on his face, listening to music on headphones (Fig. 1). He is absorbed in the music; he taps his foot and bobs his head in time to it. And yet he is not completely taken up with it, for he is also thinking about what and who he wants to be (the words we hear aren't being spoken out loud by anyone, they are in the young man's head—something which the musical context makes seem natural, for when you listen to music you seem to leave the world of people and things, and enter one of thought and feeling. Or at least, that is *one* of the many experiences that music has to offer.)

Later in the commercial the young man appears as a musician. There is one episode where he is playing with his band, backed by two attractive girls (Fig. 2). Everything is lurex and sequins; this is glamour, this is the real thing, this is what being a musician is all about . . . But the sequence is no more than a fantasy (you can tell this because, unlike

Figs. 1–3. Stills from a Prudential commercial

the rest of the commercial, it is shot in black and white), and the picture dissolves into a scene in a shopping mall— Whitley's shopping centre in Bayswater, to be precise (Fig. 3). The young man is still there, but his electronic keyboard has turned into a piano—and the pretty girls have turned into old women. One asks 'Do you know "I want to be Bobby's girl"?' 'Oh no,' mutters our hero, now fully back in reality, as he settles down to play the woman's request.

You could think of television commercials as a massive experiment into musical meaning. Advertisers use music to communicate meanings that would take too long to put into words, or that would carry no conviction in them. The Prudential commercial uses music as a powerful symbol for aspiration, self-fulfilment, the desire to 'be what you want to be', as the voice-over says. More than that, it uses a particular sort of music—rock music—to target a particular segment of society, the twenty- or maybe thirty-somethings. (The commercial is advertising pension plans that you can take with you from one job to another, and obviously they are of interest to people near the beginning of their careers. It is basically saying that you will probably try a number of jobs before you find the right one, and you need a pension plan that you can take with you from one job to another.) But there is something unusual about the way it does this. For while you *see* rock music—the young man tapping his foot as he listens to his Walkman, the band—you don't *hear* it. Instead, you hear music in a watered-down version of what is sometimes called the 'common-practice' style, the style of Western European art music from the eighteenth to the early twentieth century: the music that record shops file under 'Classical', and that books on music traditionally refer to simply as 'music', as if there were no other kind.

The meaning of the commercial emerges out of this odd juxtaposition of the music you see and the music you hear.

Rock stands for youth, freedom, being true to yourself; in a word, authenticity. Classical music, by contrast, encodes maturity and, by extension, the demands of responsibility to family and to society. Through music, the commercial accomplishes a kind of conjuring trick, combining both sets of values and in this way selling the advertiser's message (you need to start planning for your old age *now*) to a segment of society that might be expected to be resistant to it; what the commercial is saying (though not in so many words, of course) is that you can begin responsible financial planning without selling out on your youth, freedom, and spontaneity. With its reassuring sonorities and controlled pacing (there are four balanced, unhurried phrases, the last culminating at the point where the Prudential logo appears on the screen), the music tells you that you're safe in Prudential's hands. But what I want to emphasize is not so much the way in which this particular commercial uses this particular music to convey meaning and value, but rather what it is about music that enables it to be used this way—which is as much as to say, what it is about music that makes it *matter* to us in the way it does.

You might define music as humanly generated sounds that are good to listen to, and that are so for themselves and not merely for the message they convey. (The first part of that formulation excludes the sighing of the wind or the singing of birds, while the second is meant to eliminate speech—though, to be sure, we do sometimes speak of the 'musical' qualities of oratory or poetry.) But the Prudential commercial makes it obvious just how much more, or maybe it would be better to say 'other', music is than good things to listen to. You only need to hear a second or two of music in a commercial to know what kind of music it is, what genre (classical, trad jazz, heavy metal, house) is being referenced, what sort of associations and connotations it brings with it. (I don't mean that everyone can *say* that the music is heavy metal or house or whatever, but that you somehow know that the music goes with fast food or financial institutions or whatever the commercial is about—or, if it doesn't, that it is being used ironically.) Of course, this requires the kind of familiarity that comes from growing up in a particular culture. A Japanese businessman watching a commercial in his London or New York hotel room will miss out on some of these associations, as will a British or American visitor to Tokyo. They will hear the same music in the commercials, but they will hear it as little more than good things to listen to. And that is only half of what music is.

Because music and its associations vary substantially from place to place (like clothes used to and food still does, just about), it functions as a symbol of national or regional identity; émigré communities sometimes cling tenaciously to their traditional music in order to preserve their identity in a foreign country. (Examples include the eastern European and Chinese communities of North America.) But national identity is by no means the only kind of identity that music helps to construct. Music, in the shape of rhythm 'n' blues and rock 'n' roll, played a central role in the creation of the youth culture of the 1960s, the so-called 'youthquake', when for the first time European and American teenagers began to adopt a lifestyle and a system of values consciously opposed to that of their parents. Music created a bond of solidarity between the members of the 'youth generation', as they called themselves, and at the same time excluded older generations. The same thing happens nowadays, only at a more subtle level: the rapid turnover of popular music styles means that only those who listen to the music stations or read the magazines know who's in and who's out, and the effect is to create a gulf between those who belong and those who don't. And nowadays it isn't just a question of the 'youth generation' versus the rest; today's urban, Western or

Westernized society has fragmented into any number of distinct, if overlapping, subcultures, each with a musical identity of its own. In today's world, deciding what music to listen to is a significant part of deciding and announcing to people not just who you 'want to be', as the Prudential commercial has it, but who you *are*.

'Music' is a very small word to encompass something that takes as many forms as there are cultural or subcultural identities. And like all small words, it brings a danger with it. When we speak of 'music', we are easily led to believe that there is *something* that corresponds to that word—something 'out there', so to speak, just waiting for us to give it a name. But when we speak of music we are really talking about a multiplicity of activities and experiences; it is only the fact that we call them all 'music' that makes it seem obvious that they belong together. (There are cultures which don't have a word for 'music' in the way that English does—so that there are different 'musics' associated with different musical instruments, say, or so that music isn't distinguished from what we would call dance or theatre.) Moreover, there is a clear hierarchy in that we regard some of these experiences and activities as more 'musical' than others. That is one of the things that the Prudential commercial plays on. The young man at the beginning is listening to music, but that isn't good enough; he wants to be *a musician*. (There are societies where this distinction wouldn't be intelligible, such as the Suyá Indians of Brazil, but in modern Western society being a musician is different from being someone who just listens to music.) As the commercial makes all too poignantly clear, though, there are musicians and musicians. For the young man doesn't want to be just a shopping-mall pianist; he wants to be a *real* musician—someone who not only plays before an appreciative, perhaps adulating, public but also plays the music *he* wants to play, his own music, and not what some old woman has asked him to.

Authenticity in Music

All this is tapping into a rich seam of musical meaning. I said that the Prudential commercial was all about authenticity—about being true to yourself even as you grow up and take your place in society (and buy a Prudential pension plan, of course). That is why it is based on rock music, for the idea of authenticity is built deep into our thinking about rock, into the meaning that it has for us. This goes back to the origins of rock in the blues, and specifically in the blues as they were played and sung by Black Americans in the deep South. The blues were seen as the authentic expression of an oppressed race, a music that came from the heart (or 'soul', as in the later music of that name), in contrast to the starched formality of the classical 'art' tradition—concert music and opera—that had been imported from Europe. But the idea that some music is natural, while other music is artificial, is a much older one. It is associated particularly with Jean-Jacques Rousseau (the same Rousseau whose writings form part of the prehistory of the French Revolution), who criticized the artificial and contrived nature of the French music of his day; Italian music by comparison, he said, was free and natural, giving direct expression to emotion and feeling.

This idea has taken many shapes in American popular culture. A representative example, which you could almost believe to have been based on Rousseau, is an episode of 'The Ghost of Faffner Hall' (a feature-length spin-off from Jim Henson's 'The Muppet Show') that included an encounter between Ry Cooder, the legendary blues-rock guitarist and singer, and a virtuoso violinist of the European tradition, Piginini. Despite his prodigious technique, the porcine celebrity has a fatal flaw: he can only play scales, and besides, he cannot play without a score in front of him. All this has not surprisingly brought on a sudden crisis of confidence, and it is at this point that Cooder, playing the part of a janitor, discovers

Piginini cowering in a broom-cupboard. How, Piginini asks, is he to satisfy his audience, who demand that instead of scales he plays all the 'little black notes' in different orders—'all piggley-higgley', as he puts it; who, in a word, demand *music*? And so Ry Cooder gives him a lesson in playing from the heart, in letting it come naturally—in *real* music, that is to say, rather than the exercise of artifice. (Real music, it turns out, sounds remarkably like the blues.)

Against such a background, it is hardly surprising that critical commentary on popular music—I am thinking in particular of heavy metal—concentrates overwhelmingly on its visceral and counter-cultural qualities, glossing over the extent to which it borrows from the classical art tradition. (Heavy metal guitarists like Edward Van Halen and Randy Rhoads have been heavily influenced by baroque composers such as Vivaldi and Johann Sebastian Bach, and such influences go back at least as far as Deep Purple and Emerson, Lake, and Palmer—not to mention Procul Harum's 'A Whiter Shade of Pale'.) But the idea of authenticity in popular music does not revolve just around the opposition with 'art' music. It has a directly ethical side, which derives largely from the commercialization of the blues—or to be more precise, its urban derivative, rhythm 'n' blues—in the 1950s and 1960s. These were the years when for the first time the American recording and broadcasting companies saw the potential for marketing Black music to White audiences. Instead of simply marketing the recordings of the Black artists themselves, however, they had the songs re-recorded by White musicians. Rock 'n' roll was in effect the White version of rhythm 'n' blues (and the outstanding example was, of course, the 'King of Rock', Elvis Presley).

By 'covering' the songs, as such re-recording was known, the recording and broadcasting companies avoided paying royalties to the original artists. As the Black rights movement gained momentum, a scandal developed over this, and the whole idea of the cover version became disreputable. As a result the development of rock music, and particularly of progressive rock, became closely associated with the idea that there was something dishonest about playing music that wasn't your own, something that went beyond questions of whether or not you had paid your copyright dues: bands were expected to write their own music and develop their own style. And above all, they were expected to come together naturally, rather than being put together by the entrepreneurs of the music business. Rock aficionados of the mid-1960s were disgusted at the success of The Monkees, an American group (modelled rather too transparently on the Beatles) which was effectively invented, and heavily promoted, by NBC-TV; they were seen as a synthetic band, an artificial construction, and thus a transgression against the very principle of authenticity.

And the same system of values remains broadly intact today. Popular music critics generally ignore the 'look-alike' bands whose aim is to mimic the sound and look of the great bands of the past, rather than developing a style of their own. They are suspicious, at best, of the Spice Girls (Fig. 4), whose meteoric rise to fame in the mid-1990s showed how it is possible to manufacture success in popular music provided you have the right formula. (Fig. 5 shows the advertisement in *The Stage* that brought the Spice Girls together.) And in a famous case, Milli Vanilli were stripped of their 1990 Gramophone award for Best New Act when it came to light that they did not actually perform any of the music on their records—a perverse judgement, arguably, in view of the extent to which modern studio technology has rendered the very concept of 'performance' problematic, at least as it has been traditionally understood. But something more complex is at work here than an anachronistic belief that music should be naturally rather than artificially produced, the product of personal sincerity rather than industry acumen.

When the Pet Shop Boys first toured in the late 1980s, by which time their recordings had already brought them

Fig. 4. Phenomenon of 1996: the Spice Girls

international success, their staged performances made it very clear that they could not re-create the sound of their studio recordings. What is more, they were up front about it; Neil Tennant, their lead singer, told *Rolling Stone* magazine, 'I quite like proving we *can't* cut it live'. And he added: 'We're a pop group, not a rock 'n' roll group.' Now what is particularly telling about this last comment is that it is generally rock musicians who draw the distinction between themselves and pop musicians, and they do so as a means of disparagement. Expressed a bit crudely (but then it *is* a bit crude), the thinking goes like this. Rock musicians perform live, create their own music, and forge their own identities; in short, they control their own destinies. Pop musicians, by contrast, are the puppets of the music business, cynically or naïvely pandering to popular tastes, and performing music composed and arranged by others; they lack authenticity, and as such they come at the bottom of the hierarchy of musicianship. To put

Fig. 5. The original advertisement for the Spice Girls (*The Stage*)

it another way, the hierarchy of musicianship elevates the originators of music—the authors, if you like—above those whose role is merely one of reproduction, in other words, the performers.

With the reissue of the masterpieces of rock on CD in the late 1980s and early 1990s (predominantly to thirty- and forty-somethings whose original vinyl recordings had long since worn out), a new strain of critical writing came into being, the aim of which was to justify the masterwork status of the classic bands' albums. It did this by showing how these bands did not simply reproduce existing music, but forged new styles and new compositions of their own on the basis of a unique vision shared by the band members. The music expressed this vision, not audience tastes or industry demand; the bands were genuine authors, in other words. But this kind of critical interpretation does a fair amount of violence to the facts. Relationships between the classic bands and the music industry were often problematic, but they were certainly close. And the distinction between authorship and reproduction is a very slippery one (doesn't a performer like Madonna stamp her own identity on a song like 'Material Girl', make it her own, regardless of who wrote it?). In a way, it is the very difficulty of sustaining the distinction between an 'authentic' rock music and an 'inauthentic' pop music that is most revealing, because it shows how determined critics have been to draw it against the odds. But what has motivated this kind of commentary on popular music? What, to adopt a useful current term, is the 'cultural work' that it is intended to accomplish?

In the next chapter I shall provide a historical context for this kind of thinking, but first I want to show how it links with the way we think about classical music. You only have to scan the music magazines on your nearest news-stand to see how thinking about classical music centres on the idea of the 'great' musician, defined as an artist whose technical skill is taken for granted, but whose artistry lies in his or her (but usually his) personal vision. The record companies' advertisements do not in general sell Beethoven or Mahler as such; like motor manufacturers (whose commercials are all about personal style because their products are practically indistinguishable), the record companies are primarily engaged in brand marketing. So what they sell is the interpretive vision of the exceptional, charismatic performer: Pollini's interpretation of Beethoven, or Rattle's interpretation of Mahler. There is a sense, then, in which it is the performer and not the music that is sold.

In this way, the classical music industry markets the great interpreters in their role of originators, or 'authors', rather than mere reproducers of music, and so upholds the same values of authenticity that are found in popular music. But it is in books on classical music that the distinction between authors and reproducers is to be found in its most literal form. For the most part, they refer to 'music' but are actually about composers and their works; if you look at the two capacious volumes of the *New Oxford Companion to Music*, for instance, you will find a mass of information on even the most obscure composers, but performers are conspicuous by their absence. It is like the role of servants in Victorian society: they have to be there, but you don't have to talk about them. (When such books do mention performers, it is as often as not in the context of a complaint at their unwarranted 'licence' or 'extravagance' in obscuring the original music through over-interpretation or gratuitous virtuosity.) And even within the select world of the composer, the same value system operates: academic writing on music almost invariably emphasizes the innovators, the creators of tradition, the Beethovens and Schoenbergs, at the expense of the many more conservative composers who write within the framework of an established style.

A value system is in place within our culture, then, which places innovation above tradition, creation above reproduction, personal expression above the market-place. In a word, music must be authentic, for otherwise it is hardly music at all.

Words and Music

I referred earlier to the 'cultural work' accomplished by critical commentary on music: by books, by magazines and newspaper reviews, by television and radio programmes, and by concert-interval conversation. Words do work because they do not simply reflect how things are. We do work with words by using them to change things, to *make* things the way they are. Or to put it more abstractly, language constructs reality rather than merely reflecting it. And this means that the languages we use of music, the stories that we tell about it, help to determine what music is—what we mean by it, and what it means to us. The values wrapped up in the idea of authenticity, for example, are not simply there in the music; they are there because the way we think about music puts them there, and of course the way we think about music also affects the way we make music, and so the process becomes circular. It is this kind of continuity in thinking about things that creates what we call 'traditions', whether in music or anything else.

The main message of this book is that we have inherited from the past a way of thinking about music that cannot do justice to the diversity of practices and experiences which that small word, 'music', signifies in today's world. When a book published by Oxford University Press a hundred years ago referred to 'music', the term had a stability of reference that it no longer has. 'Music' meant the European art tradition focused on such masters as J. S. Bach, Beethoven, and Brahms (the role in music history played by the letter 'B' has

never been satisfactorily explained); there were historical an-
tecedents to this tradition, and there were also quaint and
sometimes unexpectedly sophisticated musical practices
found elsewhere in the world, but the concept of 'music' was
firmly rooted in a specific corpus of musical works, and
through that in a specific time and place.

But as that curious word 'works' suggests, this reflected
something deeper than just the Eurocentricism of Western
culture in the century preceding the First World War. It
reflected what underlay that culture: the classic industrial
economy, based on the *production of goods* which were
subsequently *distributed* and finally *consumed* by the public
who purchased them. (This is a very different type of economy from the late twentieth-century service economy, based
not on manufactured goods but on such 'products' as the pension plans in the Prudential commercial.) In the same way,
music was thought of as being based on the *production of
compositions* which were subsequently *performed* and finally
experienced (enjoyed, appreciated) by the listening public.
Musical culture, in short, was seen as a process of creating,
distributing, and consuming what became known around the
beginning of the nineteenth century as 'works' of music. The
term is a revealing one because it creates a direct link with
the world of economics. One of the basic principles of capi-
talism is that you can in effect stockpile labour—either by
accumulating the products of labour, or by accumulating
something else (most obviously money) that you can exchange for labour. In the same way, the musical 'work' gave a
permanent form to music; music was no longer to be thought
of as purely evanescent, an activity or experience that fades
into the past as soon as it is over. For while performances of
musical works take place in time, the work itself endures. (As
Jean-Paul Sartre once put it, if the concert hall burns down
during a performance of Beethoven's Seventh Symphony,
that is not the end of the symphony.) And in this way music

becomes something you can stockpile or accumulate, a form of what might be termed 'aesthetic capital'. We don't normally call it that, however; we call it 'the repertory', of which more in Chapter 2.

The three categories I have just mentioned (production, distribution, consumption) bear a close resemblance to those on which the British National Curriculum and GCSE (General Certificate of Secondary Education) syllabus are based: composing, performing, and appraising. ('Appraising' might be defined as listening plus thinking, with a measure of evaluation thrown in, although the definition is a dubious one since listening always includes an element of thinking and evaluation.) The curriculum authorities use the present participle rather than the noun—'composing' rather than 'composition'—in order to convey that these are activities in which students can engage during the course of their studies; this is part of the participant ethos of contemporary music education, which stresses the act of composing rather than the study and appreciation of the works of the great composers. (A generation earlier the idea of school students composing was almost unknown; at most they might *imitate* the simpler works of certain approved masters.) And the fact that the curriculum is divided into these three activities—composing, performing, and appraising—is meant to indicate that each of them is something that any student can be expected to do, just as everybody can be expected to read and write.

But the basic facts of language run counter to this democratic and integrative urge; the taxonomy of composing/performing/appraising ends up perpetuating the very distinctions it was designed to erase. It is not just that turning music back into an activity rather than a form of aesthetic capital, as I called it, is more than can be achieved just by substituting 'composing' for 'composition'. It is in the nature of things that the activities of composing, performing, and appraising represent a chronological sequence (you can't perform something until it's been composed, and most people can't appraise it until it's been performed). And what begins as a chronological priority somehow turns into a hierarchy of value—a hierarchy that is reinforced by the way it maps on to different individuals or social groups: composers, performers, and the 'appraisers' who range from professional music critics and educators to music-lovers and 'ordinary' listeners ('ordinary', that is, in the sense that they are not musicians). At the same time, though, there are repertories in which the three terms can't be sensibly differentiated (composition and performance in the case of studio-generated dance music, say). In all these ways the National Curriculum/GCSE terminology gives, at most, a new gloss on old thinking.

There is, in short, a nexus of interrelated assumptions built into the basic language we use of music: that musicianship is the preserve of appropriately qualified specialists; that innovation (research and design) is central to musical culture; that the key personnel in musical culture are the composers who generate what might be termed the core product; that performers are in essence no more than middlemen, apart from those exceptional interpreters who acquire a kind of honorary composer's status; and that listeners are consumers, playing an essentially passive role in the cultural process that, in economic terms, they underpin. But because these assumptions are built into our language we can't easily talk about them; we can't even see them for what they are. In a word, they are transparent. They seem natural in the same way that the blues seem natural—or that the market economy seems natural, or the way we cook. But in truth none of these things are natural; they are all human constructions, products of culture, and accordingly they vary from time to time and from place to place. It is one of music's special characteristics that it appears to be a product of nature—that it appears, in a widely used phrase, to be a 'universal language'—but, in reality, this appearance is an illusion. And so, in Chapter 2, I shall show how the kind of assumptions I have been talking about, and the kind of musical values to which they give rise, are by no means universal, but are rather the product of a particular time and place, and not our own.

2 Back to Beethoven

Joy through Suffering

The time to which I referred at the end of the last chapter is the early nineteenth century, and the place is Europe, or to be more precise the musical capitals of northern and central Europe (in particular London, Paris, Berlin, and Vienna). This is the period during which the capitalist model of production, distribution, and consumption became fully embedded in society; across Europe it was a time of urbanization, with a large proportion of the population migrating from the countryside in search of industrial employment, while within the cities the middle classes (or bourgeoisie) occupied a steadily increasing economic, political, and cultural role. In the arts—which in this context means primarily literature, painting, and music—the most important development of the period was what might be termed the construction of bourgeois subjectivity. By this I mean that they explored and celebrated the inner world of feeling and emotion; music, in particular, turned away from the world and became dedicated to personal expression. (Better than any verbal explanation of this is the painting in Fig. 6.) Because of its ability to present feeling and emotion directly, without the intervention of

Fig. 6. Fernand Khnopff, *Listening to Schumann*, 1883, oil on canvas, Brussels, Musées Royeaux des Beaux-Arts de Belgique

words or depicted objects, music came to occupy a privileged role within Romanticism, as the new mood across the arts was known.

Carl Dahlhaus, the German musicologist whose writings became enormously influential in the 1980s, characterized the early nineteenth century as the age of Beethoven and Rossini. And those who lived at the time were no doubt conscious of other voices, too. But it is Beethoven's voice that has dominated thinking about music since then; for generations, finding your voice as a composer meant defining yourself in relation to Beethoven. (Fifty years later, Brahms spoke of hearing the tread of a giant behind him.) The turning away from the world to which I referred, then, can be seen in Beethoven's refusal to take a secure, salaried position (like Bach, who was the organist of St Thomas's Church in Leipzig, or Haydn, who was master of music for a feudal landowner in what is now Hungary). It can also be seen in Beethoven's insistence on writing the music he wanted to write when he wanted to write it; again there is a contrast with the cantatas that Bach was contracted to write for his church for performance on specific dates, or the music that Haydn was required to produce for set occasions. But most of all it can be seen in the nature of the *music* that Beethoven wrote: in its constant subversion of conventional expectations, in its striving after heroic effect or passionate intimacy, in the way that it was experienced as speaking directly to each listener as an individual. Something of this experience can be glimpsed in a drawing by Eugène Louis Lami entitled 'Upon hearing a Beethoven symphony' (Fig. 7). The listeners may be physically in a single room, but each of them is wrapped up in a different, private world. Music has taken them out of the public world of people and things, as I said of the young man in the Prudential commercial; indeed, for all practical purposes, the people in Lami's drawing might as well be listening on headphones.

A much later composer, Anton Webern, once described a bad performance of one of his own compositions as a high note followed by a low note—'the music of a madman', he added disconsolately. Much of Beethoven's music seems to have struck its early listeners in the same way, although they expressed it differently. Giuseppe Cambini, for instance, wrote of Beethoven's first two symphonies:

Now he takes the majestic flight of the eagle; then he creeps along grotesque paths. After penetrating the soul with a sweet melancholy he soon tears it by a mass of barbaric chords. He seems to harbour doves and crocodiles at the same time.

Fig. 7. Eugène Louis Lami, *Upon hearing a Beethoven symphony*, 1840, watercolour, present whereabouts unknown

Cambini's picturesque comments turn on the abruptness, the discontinuity, the contradiction from one moment to the next that distinguished Beethoven's music from that of his predecessors (most famously Haydn and Mozart). And if his comment about majestic flight and grotesque creeping in effect paraphrases Webern's 'a high note, a low note', some at least of Beethoven's listeners went on to draw the same disconsolate conclusion: that they were listening to the music of a madman, or at least of a great composer whose regrettable deafness had distorted his musical imagination and, perhaps, unbalanced his mind.

If it had been an unheard-of young composer who presented the Viennese public of the 1820s with the Ninth Symphony or the 'Hammerklavier' Sonata, they would almost certainly have been dismissed as bizarre and incompetent. (The Ninth Symphony set tradition on its head by introducing voices, while the 'Hammerklavier' Sonata was unplayable by contemporary standards.) But by the time that Beethoven composed these works—which he never heard, for his deafness was by then profound—the musical public had a massive emotional investment in his music; he was acknowledged throughout Europe as the greatest composer of his day, and perhaps that the world had ever known. And so his many devotees set themselves to work at understanding his music in a way that audiences had perhaps never worked at understanding music before.

The result was a flood of critical commentary that aimed to explain the apparent incoherence of the music by demonstrating some kind of underlying plot or narrative, in relation to which its superficially grotesque properties could be seen as logical or at least comprehensible. Franz Joseph Fröhlich, for instance, saw the first movement of the Ninth Symphony as a kind of self-portrait in music, with its kaleidoscopic sequence of contrasted sonorities representing the contradictory emotions that made up Beethoven's complex personality. And he saw the symphony as a whole as depicting Beethoven's struggle to overcome the devastating blow of his deafness; the final movement, with its setting of Schiller's 'Ode to Joy', represents Beethoven's victory over his affliction, Fröhlich said, and more generally the power of joy to overcome suffering. In this way Beethoven's deafness was turned to interpretive advantage. It became, so to speak, a key that unlocked the hidden meaning of the music, giving the listener direct access to the composer's message and so creating a deeper understanding than could ever have been gained by a mere casual listening.

Joy through suffering: this phrase (extracted from one of Beethoven's letters, where it actually referred to an uncomfortable coach journey) became the central motto of the Beethoven cult that was promulgated in the first half of the twentieth century by the French writer Romain Rolland. Rolland held Beethoven up as a role model for a less heroic age, epitomizing personal sincerity, altruism, and self-denial —in a word, authenticity. The results of Rolland's lifelong advocacy can still be seen in the special role which the image of Beethoven in general, and the Ninth Symphony in particular, occupies in today's world: as the supranational anthem of the European Union (though it is only the tune of the 'Ode to Joy', not the words, that are officially recognized in Brussels); as the work chosen for a special Christmas concert marking the demolition of the Berlin Wall (for which the word 'Joy' was replaced by 'Freedom', so that the last movement became an Ode to Freedom); as the work which marks the year's end in Japan, where massed performances take place in sports stadiums, sometimes with choirs of thousands. (Rolland's little book *Beethoven*, the bible of the Beethoven cult, was translated into Japanese in the 1920s.) The Ninth Symphony has even penetrated popular culture through such films as *A Clockwork Orange* and *Die Hard*, as well as through any number of cover versions of the 'Ode to Joy'.

Siding with the Angels

The Beethoven cult, then, whose origins lie early in the nineteenth century but which shows little sign of abating as it enters the new millenium, is a (perhaps the) central pillar in the culture of classical music. Not surprisingly, then, many of the ideas most deeply embedded in our thinking about music today can be traced back to the ferment of ideas that surrounded the reception of Beethoven's music. In this section I focus on two of these ideas: the relationships of authority which permeate musical culture, and the power of music to transcend boundaries of time and space.

The concept of music being a kind of commodity naturally gives the composer a position of centrality, as the generator of the core product. But the idea which developed during the early reception of Beethoven's music, that to listen to it was in some sense to be in direct communion with the composer himself, added another dimension that can be best expressed through a cluster of etymologically related words. First there is the role of the composer as *author* or originator of the music. This is the source of the *authority* that attaches to the composer, for example when performers like Roger Norrington claim that their interpretations represent Beethoven's real intentions, or when editors claim the same for their *authoritative* editions. (The authority of the performance or edition is in other words borrowed, a reflection of the composer's authority—as is made explicit when the composer *authorizes* a particular version or realization of the music.) And finally, this authority can easily turn into *authoritarianism*, an attribute perhaps most notoriously seen in the relationship between conductors and orchestral musicians, but arguably built into our thinking about performance in general.

It was said in the nineteenth century of Hans von Bülow's playing of Beethoven's piano music that as a performer he effaced himself: when you listened, you were conscious only of Beethoven, not of Bülow. (The record cover in Fig. 8 seems to be saying the same; note, again, the Beethoven connection.) What is telling is that this was, and is, said by way of high praise, as if the best performers are the ones of whom you are not even aware. The same, of course, might be said of waiters in the best restaurants. What is more, performers traditionally wear the same clothes as waiters: dinner-jackets. I do not mean this as a simply frivolous observation. The point I am making is that the way we think about music leads us to assign a subordinate status to the performer—a status that is totally at odds with the adulation of charismatic

Fig. 8. Cover from Solomon's recording of Beethoven's 'Emperor' Concerto (HMV ALP 1300)

performers in the market-place—and that this is confirmed by its links with other expressions of subordinate status within society. Or to put it another way, the idea that the performer's role is to reproduce what the composer has created builds an authoritarian power structure into musical culture, whether expressed in the relationship between composer and performer or in relationships between performers— especially, as I said, between the conductor (who acts as the composer's representative) and the rank-and-file orchestral players. All in all, then, the performer occupies a conflicted and inadequately theorized role within musical culture, and I shall repeatedly come back to this.

So much for the hierarchy of value as between composing and performing, the first two terms of the National Curriculum/GCSE taxonomy of music. What of the third term, appraising? Here, perhaps, the charge of authoritarianism becomes even more apt. As individual (and individualistic) interpretations like Fröhlich's congealed into critical traditions, and as music education became increasingly focused round schools, conservatories, and universities, so the correct way to listen to music became more and more narrowly prescribed. Courses in 'music appreciation' taught students and music-lovers to link what they heard in the music with biographical facts about the composer or historical information about the development of musical style; it trained them to listen out for musical structure, for example registering the first theme, second theme, development section, and recapitulation that define the classical 'sonata' form. Such courses became (and in some places remain) the basis of class teaching of music at school level, and have long had a strong presence within liberal arts education in North America.

What is perhaps more important than the specifics of this kind of music teaching is the general attitude towards musical listening that it inculcates: you should listen attentively, respectfully, in a detached manner (avoiding being too caught up in the sensory or emotional ebb and flow of the music), and informed by appropriate knowledge. Subjected to the authority of the music educator (an authority again borrowed from the composer), the listener—the 'ordinary' listener—is positioned firmly at the bottom of the musical hierarchy. Such thinking about music meshed in with the authoritarian structures that dominated education as a whole until well into the postwar period, and one of the main intentions underlying the music provisions of the National Curriculum and GCSE was to counterbalance this impoverished view of the listener's role in music. Instead of passively 'appreciating' the great music of the past, students were, and are, encouraged to take music literally into their own hands, linking appraising back into composing and performing. As I said, however, this attempt to empower the individual is not well served by the ways of thinking about music which we have inherited from the age of Beethoven.

Beethoven's deafness makes a good starting-point for the second of the ideas I referred to: the power of music to transcend boundaries of time and space. In the mythology that has grown up in the 170 years since Beethoven's death, his deafness has come to occupy a role that goes far beyond its curiosity value (though this is a value that should not be underestimated, as the spectacular example of the deaf percussionist Evelyn Glennie demonstrates). This is because it acts as a potent symbol of Beethoven's independence of, or alienation from, the society in which he lived: reduced to communication with the outside world via conversation books, in which visitors wrote down their half of the conversation while Beethoven spoke his, the composer dissociated himself from worldly concerns such as the pursuit of social or financial success and devoted himself solely to his muse. Or so you would think from much of the myth-making iconography and literature that surrounds Beethoven. (Fig. 9, taken from the original 1938 edition of *The Oxford Companion to Music*, is a representative example.) But the truth was rather different, as Beethoven's publishers and creditors knew to their cost, while Maynard Solomon's biography of Beethoven has demonstrated the role that the composer's sometimes bizarre social aspirations played in his psychological make-up.

The distortions that make up the Beethoven myth are as significant as the truth that underlies them, because they reflect the values and concerns of the myth-makers. One of the most consistent of these distortions is the claim that

BEETHOVEN NEARS THE END

By Batt

HE is seen in his workroom in the old Schwarzspanierhaus. Behind him stands his Graf piano, wrecked by his frantic efforts to hear his own playing. Odd coins lie scattered among the litter on the table. There are his ear-trumpets, his conversation books—in which any visitor would have to write what he wished to say—with a carpenter's pencil, letters, quill pens, a broken coffee cup, remnants of food and his candlestick.

The squalid disorder meant nothing to him in those days. He had finished with the world. Since 1824 the medium of the string quartet had absorbed his mind to the exclusion of all else and now, stone-deaf, very ill but still indomitable, he rose to heights which even he had never reached before. His stormy life closed with a revelation which, in the last five quartets, was the crowning glory of his achievement.   B.

Fig. 9. 'Beethoven nears the end', by Batt (Oswald Barrett)

Beethoven was a misunderstood genius whose music was not valued in his own day; critical accounts of the first performance of the Ninth Symphony, for example, constantly play down its considerable success, despite what appears to have been a fairly shambolic performance. This distortion accomplishes two kinds of cultural work. The first relates, once again, to authenticity: lack of popular acclaim demonstrates Beethoven's authenticity through his refusal to pander to popular tastes and give the public what it wanted. (This has a parallel in Beethoven's own disparaging of Rossini, whom he saw as giving the public precisely what it wanted, and nothing more.) The second is the construction of a privileged viewpoint from which we can see what Beethoven's original audiences failed to see: the intrinsic value of his music, which he wrote not for his own time but for all time. And it has to be said that for us, the inheritors and upholders of the Beethoven myth, this is an attractive way to view the music of the past, because it makes our understanding of Beethoven's music superior to that of his contemporaries. With the benefit of hindsight, we invariably find ourselves on the side of the angels.

Integral to the Beethoven myth, then, and to the way of thinking about music that it epitomizes, is the idea of music as aesthetic capital—music that can be laid down, like fine wine, for future enjoyment. Beethoven was one of the first composers specifically known to have thought about the role that his music might continue to play after his own death; towards the end of his life he tried without success to interest a number of publishers in the idea of a complete and authoritative edition of his works which would rectify the mistakes in existing editions and represent his final intentions. (He was also one of the first composers to use the sobriquet 'work' selectively, giving his major compositions 'Opus' numbers—the Ninth Symphony, for instance, is Op. 125—while omitting his more ephemeral productions.) But it was in the years after Beethoven's death that a new and powerful metaphor came into play which can be seen as underpinning the idea of music as aesthetic capital. This was the metaphor of the musical museum.

To be sure, 'musical museum' was not a term in common use by nineteenth-century musicians and critics, though in 1835 the virtuoso pianist and composer Franz Liszt called for the foundation of just such an institution. In the visual arts (which have often been a source of thinking subsequently applied to music), however, the idea of the museum coalesced into its present-day form at just this period. These were the years in which the great public collections of antiquities, paintings, decorative arts, and ethnographic objects came into being. Such collections, available for the enjoyment or edification of the populace at large, aimed to bring together the finest works of all times and places. The objects in them were abstracted from their original conditions of use and valorization, and were instead to be judged on a single, universal criterion of intrinsic beauty. (There is an obvious linkage between this and contemporary colonialism; the objects in question often came from the colonies, while the supposedly universal criteria of beauty were in fact those of their rulers.) And all this forms the backdrop for the formation of what Lydia Goehr has called 'the imaginary museum of musical works', in which the music of the past was to be displayed as a permanent, if invisible, collection.

The fact that this museum did not actually exist—that it was imaginary—in no way detracts from its significance; it provided the conceptual framework within which music took its place in the cultural heritage. What classical musicians call 'the repertory' (or 'the canon') is, in effect, the music that was selected for inclusion in the musical museum. Since Beethoven's time it has been the normal expectation that great music should continue to be performed long after the composer's death; that is largely what 'great' means. But before then, this was very much the exception. Even Bach's music dropped out of performance for the best part of a century and had to be revived, in the almost literal sense of breathing new life into old notes. (It is no accident that this revival began within a few years of Beethoven's death.) And as the musical museum came into being, as musical works ceased to grow old and musical time began to stand still, so the term 'classical music' came into common currency. Borrowed from the 'classical' art of Greece and Rome, which was seen as the expression of universal standards of beauty, this term implied that similar standards had now been set in music, against which the production of all other times and places must be measured.

The Spirit Realm

In his essay on Mozart's G minor Symphony, Heinrich Schenker wrote that the music of the geniuses is 'removed from the generations and their tides'. Schenker was active as a pianist and teacher in Vienna during the first three decades of the twentieth century, but his current fame in academic circles dates from after the Second World War, when the system of musical analysis which he developed became more and more widely used in conservatories and university music departments. (To cram it into a single sentence, Schenker showed how most compositions of the classical tradition could be understood as based on the model of a single musical phrase that is massively expanded by a series of elaborations; his system of analysis essentially consists of stripping the elaborations away from the music, so reducing it to the underlying model.) Many threads of nineteenth- and twentieth-century thinking about music intersect in his writings, and it is for this reason that I introduce them here. The geniuses to whom Schenker refers are of course the composers whose works have been admitted to the musical museum, and Schenker is saying that their works endure independently of the time and place in which they originated; they inhabit an unchanging, immaterial domain of their own.

Schenker's belief that music represents an incursion into the human world of some higher form of reality was quite literal. 'Music', he says (and this is Music with a capital 'M'), uses the genius composer 'as a medium, so to speak, and quite spontaneously'. For Schenker, this is the definition of a genius composer; ordinary composers simply write what they want, but in the case of the genius 'The superior force of truth—of Nature, as it were—is at work mysteriously behind his consciousness, guiding his pen, without caring in the least whether the happy artist himself wanted to do the right thing or not.' (The male gendering, incidentally, is normative in Schenker's thinking—and in traditional thinking about music in general, as will become clear in Chapter 7.) The composer speaks, then, but with a voice that is not his own: it is the voice of Nature. For Schenker, the authority of the composer—the authority delegated to conductor, editor, and teacher—is itself ultimately a reflection of a higher Author, for the value of music lies (as he put it) in 'the elevation of the spirit . . . an uplifting, of an almost religious character, to God and to the geniuses through whom he works'.

The intuition that music is a kind of window on an esoteric world that lies beyond ordinary knowledge predates the Christian era and is replicated in distant civilizations. In the West, it stems from the discovery of the Greek philosopher Pythagoras, five centuries before Christ, that the notes of the musical scale correspond to simple integer proportions (if their tensions are the same, a string half the length of another string will produce a note an octave higher, a string two-thirds of the length will produce a note a perfect fifth higher, and so on); maybe, Pythagoras and his followers speculated, the entire universe is built on the same mathematical principles, so that the music we hear is an audible version of the harmony that binds the earth and sun and stars together, the imperceptible but ever-present 'music of the spheres'. (Fig. 10 is a seventeenth-century representation of this idea.) Similar beliefs persisted for many centuries in China, where a series of earthquakes or other natural disasters would sometimes provoke an investigation into the tuning of the various notes of the scale, in case the source of the trouble was some misalignment between earthly music and its cosmic equivalent.

Common to these historically and geographically remote cultures, and others, is the idea that the plucking of a string

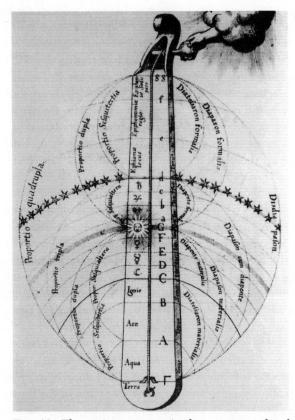

Fig. 10. The universe conceived as a monochord (from Robert Fludd, *Utriusque Cosmi Historia* (Oppenheim, 1617)). The planets and elements are shown to the left of the string, musical notes to the right; the circles show the mathematical proportions linking them. A celestial hand literally tunes the universe

Fig. 11. Cover from Kathleen Ferrier's recording of Mahler's *Das Lied von der Erde* (Decca LXT 5576)

or the sounding of a chime can give access to another plane of existence. And if nineteenth-century European writers such as E. T. A. Hoffmann echoed these ancient traditions when they spoke of music as 'the spirit realm', something of the same can be seen in such twentieth-century images as Fig. 11. It shows Kathleen Ferrier, one of the most famous British singers in the postwar period, and it demonstrates that even if the camera cannot lie, it can certainly tell a story: the artist gazes upwards and into the far distance, while light suffuses her from above, as if it were the radiance of a higher world to which her performance (and Mahler's music) can give access. What is pictured is, quite literally, an act of revelation. And though the young protagonist in the Prudential commercial listens to rock instead of Mahler, it is the same world that he glimpses, too, if his turned-away eyes and abstracted, quizzical smile are anything to go by.

Like personal stereo, records (intended primarily for domestic consumption) promote the private invocation of music's power to summon up the spirit realm. But it is in the concert hall that the most spectacular celebration of music's power is to be witnessed. The concert, as we know it today, is another invention of the nineteenth century; music was performed before audiences in previous centuries, of course, but within such contexts as courts or aristocratic homes. What was new about the nineteenth-century concert is that it was open to anyone who could afford a ticket. (That, however, still ruled out most people; it was only in the twentieth century, with the development of broadcasting and recording technology, that classical music became available to practically anyone who wanted to hear it.) And the development of the concert as an economically viable form of public entertainment gave rise to the next major development: the building of purpose-built concert halls where an audience of hundreds (or, in the case of later buildings such as the Royal Albert Hall or Chicago Auditorium, thousands) could witness the ritual which musical performance became (Fig. 12).

Today, entering a concert hall is like entering a cathedral: it is literally a rite of passage, giving access to an interior that is separated from the outside world both economically (because you have to pay to get in) and acoustically. Within the inner sanctum, a strict code of audience etiquette prevails; not only must you be quiet and remain more or less still while the music plays, but you must avoid clapping between movements, reserving your applause until the end of a complete

Fig. 12. The Auditorium, Chicago: opening night (9 December 1889)

symphony or concerto. The performers are bound by an equally strict code, ranging for instance from dress (dinner-jacket for orchestral performances, black trousers with coloured shirt for early music, and so on) to the convention that pianists (but not organists), and singers in recitals (but not oratorios), must perform from memory except in the hardest of contemporary works. Why some musicians are not expected to have as good memories as others is something of a mystery, but the convention of memorizing music is not entirely an arbitrary one: it seems to have developed in tandem with the idea that solo performance should appear to be spontaneous, that it should give the impression of an improvisation that just happens to coincide note for note with the composer's score. In other words, rather than just reproducing something you have carefully memorized, you should give the impression of being in some sense possessed by it—

and that, of course, links with the idea of music giving access to the world beyond or making audible the voice of Nature. (It also links with what goes on in rock concerts, however different other aspects of the ritual may be.)

Nineteenth-century commentators were quite conscious of what I have been seeking, in a circumspect way, to suggest: that, as conventional religion succumbed to the onslaught of science, music provided an alternative route to spiritual consolation. Indeed they sometimes talked of 'art-religion' or 'the religion of art'. And this, obviously, provides the context for the association with musicianship of the ethical qualities—personal sincerity, being true to oneself, and so forth—that I have grouped together under the term 'authenticity'. But what is most striking is the way in which another ethical quality, purity, became associated not with musicians, but with music itself. By 'pure' music, writers of the second half of the nineteenth century and the first half of the twentieth meant music which was just that, music: in other words, music that did not accompany words (like songs or opera) or tell stories (like the 'symphonic poems' of Liszt, Smetana, or Richard Strauss). Like some fly in the ointment, words were seen as sullying music, or as diluting its spiritual powers. And an extraordinary debate began, which raged for a century before fizzling out inconclusively, in which the advocates of 'pure' music attempted to demonstrate that music did not depend on words for its beauty and meaning, while the proponents of opera and music drama argued that only in conjunction with the word could music realize its full potential for signification.

What happens in the opera house is something else; within the concert hall, 'pure' music reigns supreme, in the symphonies, concertos, piano sonatas, and string quartets whose effects of intimacy, passion, and spiritual consolation are created 'by purely musical means', as the old catch-phrase of its proponents has it. And this is a legacy of the nineteenth century, for while purely instrumental music had of course existed before then, it had always been thought of as subordinate to the genres in which music accompanied words: cantata, oratorio, opera. But the victory of music against the word was a flawed one. For as the word was eliminated from music, it began to fill the space *around* music. It penetrated the inner sanctum of the concert hall in the form of the programme-note (another nineteenth-century invention), not to mention concert-interval chatter. And in the world outside it proliferated in the successive forms of the music appreciation text, record sleeve, magazine, CD-ROM, and web site. In this way, the musical world of which Beethoven laid the foundations developed not only the idea of music without words but also, and paradoxically, the basic model we retain today of how words should relate to music: by explaining it. The paradox lies in the fact that if music needs to be explained through words, then it must stand in need of explanation, must be in some sense incomplete without it; in Scott Burnham's words, 'music no longer in need of words now seems more than ever in need of words'. I shall come back to this near the end of the book.

I called this chapter 'Back to Beethoven'. But the title was perhaps a misnomer after all. For it turns out that, in our ways of thinking about music, we have never really escaped from his abiding presence.

3 A State of Crisis?

A Global Resource

Ideas of the spirit realm, of Nature or Music speaking through the genius composer, seem about as remote as they could be from musical culture at the turn of the twenty-first century. But the ways of thinking about music that accompanied the reception of Beethoven's music were all of a piece, and they are the source of the features of contemporary musical culture which I described in Chapter 1: the emphasis on authenticity and self-expression that underlies much popular music criticism, for instance, or the strangely conflicted ways in which we talk about performers in both the popular and classical traditions. And it was only a year ago, as I write, that Harrison Birtwistle (perhaps Britain's leading modernist composer) condensed the Beethovenian concept of the composer into a dozen words when he announced, 'I can't be responsible for the audience: I'm not running a restaurant.'

In fact, if the nineteenth-century idea of 'pure music' meant understanding it in its own terms, independent of any external meaning or social context, then you could argue that twentieth-century sound reproduction technology has given

a massive boost to this kind of thinking. The music of practically all times and places lies no further away than the nearest
record store; if that's too far, then internet sites like ROCK
AROUND THE WORLD will bring it into your living-room via a
modem. Chronological and geographical differences evap-
orate as we increasingly think of music as an almost infinite
pool of resources to be pulled off the shelf or downloaded
from the Web. And this might be seen as the ultimate realization of the idea of music that evolved during the early years of
the Beethoven cult, the years when the canon of classical
masterworks came into being, with major works being laid
down as cultural capital instead of going out of fashion a
generation after they were composed.

If the availability of music within today's society represents the culmination of nineteenth-century thinking in
some ways, however, in others it could hardly be more different. In Beethoven's time, and right through the century, the
only music you could hear was live music, whether in a public concert hall or a domestic parlour. (The manufacture of
upright pianos, small enough to fit into middle-class homes,
was one of the biggest growth industries from the middle of
the nineteenth century up to the First World War—as was the
publication of sheet music to go with them.) But nowadays it
is as if the imaginary museum of music is all around us. We
can watch grand opera (or the Balinese 'monkey dance',
based on the *Ramayana*) from the comfort of an armchair. We
can listen to David Bowie (or a Beethoven symphony) while
driving into work. Through personal stereo we can integrate
bebop or heavy metal into our experience of the cityscape.
And brought like this into the midst of everyday life, music
becomes an element in the definition of personal lifestyle,
alongside the choice of a new car, clothes, or perfume. Deciding whether to listen to Beethoven, or Bowie, or Balinese
music becomes the same kind of choice as deciding whether
to eat Italian, Thai, or Cajun tonight. However unpalatable to

Birtwistle, the truth is that in today's consumer society we *do* behave rather as if composers were high-class restaurateurs.

We have a paradox. On the one hand, modern technology has given music the autonomy which nineteenth-century musicians and aestheticians claimed for it (but in a sense fraudulently, because in reality 'pure music' was confined to the middle-class ambience of concert hall and home). On the other hand, it has turned many of the basic assumptions of nineteenth-century musical culture upside down. The more we behave as musical consumers, treating music as some kind of electronically mediated commodity or lifestyle accessory, the less compatible our behaviour becomes with nineteenth-century conceptions of the composer's authority. Indeed, as I suggested, the very idea of authorship has become parlous in relation to contemporary studio production, where techniques of recording and digital sound transformation place as much creative scope in the sound engineer's and producer's hands as the so-called artist's. (Many writers on music badly underestimate the contribution to the final product of sound engineers and producers.)

And the immediate availability of music from all over the world means that it has become as easy and unproblematic to talk about different 'musics' as about different 'cuisines'. For someone like Schenker, talking about 'musics' would have been preposterous: given that it is the voice of Music or Nature that we hear through the genius composers, he might have said, it makes no more sense to talk of 'musics' than it would of 'natures'. What is at issue here is the difference between a nineteenth- or early twentieth-century European mindset, according to which the achievements of Western art and science represented a kind of gold standard against which those of other times and places must be measured, and the circumstances of today's post-colonial, multicultural society. It is like the difference between believing in the advance of Civilization, and accepting that across the world there have been (and will continue to be) any number of different civilizations, each with its own system of values.

But perhaps the most telling contrast between today's musical world and the ways of thinking about it that we have inherited from the nineteeth century concerns high and low art. The very terms seem suspect today, and even if you wanted to use them it would be hard to be confident about what is high and what is low art. (Birtwistle is high art, obviously, and presumably the Spice Girls are low art, but you only have to read the rock and pop criticism columns of the Sunday papers to see how inadequate it would be simply to identify high art with the classical tradition and low art with popular music.) Writers about music in the academic tradition, however, have traditionally had no such qualms. High art, or 'art' music, meant the notation-based traditions of the leisured classes, and above all the great repertory of Bach, Beethoven, and Brahms. Low art meant everything else, that is to say the limitless variety of popular and mainly non-notated—and hence historically irretrievable—musical traditions. Some low art, according to this view, might have valuable qualities of its own, in particular the rural folksongs that scholars were busily collecting in Europe and America around the turn of the twentieth century, and that composers as various as Dvořák, Vaughan Williams, and Bartók incorporated into their own music; provided they had survived in their original form and avoided contamination by the burgeoning, urban-based music industry, such folksongs were seen as conveying something of the unspoilt national character of the countryside and its inhabitants. But that did not stop them being seen as low art, because they did not spring from the individual vision of an inspired composer. The voice of the people might be heard through them, but hardly the voice of Music.

This confident distinction between high and low art still persists in the standard format of music history or appreciation textbooks. They tell the story of Western 'art' music, focused at first on Europe and expanding in the nineteenth century to North America. And then, after the story is basically finished, they add a chapter or two on popular music (possibly tracing its history before the twentieth century, but concentrating on jazz—which has been transformed since the Second World War into a kind of alternative 'art' tradition—and rock). It is obvious that there is a kind of apartheid at work here; popular music is segregated from the 'art' tradition. What is even more revealing, however, is the treatment of non-Western traditions in such books, or even in larger multi-volume surveys such as the *New Oxford History of Music*. If such traditions appear at all, they generally come right at the beginning. A common strategy is to begin with a couple of chapters on the elements of music—scales, notation, instruments, and so forth—and bring non-Western musics into that. Or sometimes you begin with the primitive music of traditional hunting and nomadic societies and move quickly on to the sophisticated traditions of Asian music (Indian, Chinese, and Korean or Japanese, perhaps, with a side excursion to take in the gamelan or percussion orchestra music of Indonesia). Either way, around the beginning of Chapter 3 there is a kind of crashing of historical and geographical gears as the scene shifts to the cathedral of Notre-Dame in Paris, where Léonin and Pérotin—the first composers of the Western tradition whose names are known today—flourished towards the end of the twelfth century, and with these preliminaries over the real story of music (that is, Western art music) begins.

It is hardly possible to miss the implicit associations in such a scheme of non-Western cultures with beginnings, and of Western culture with progress. That such thinking was commonplace at the turn of the twentieth century, the time when the sun never set on the British Empire, is only to be expected. That it is still to be encountered at the turn of the twenty-first is astonishing, for it offers an entirely inadequate basis for understanding music in today's pluralist society. It is hard to think of another field in which quite such uncritically ethnocentric and élitist conceptions have held such sway until so recently—for, as will become clear in the final chapter of this book, since the mid-1980s a sea change has taken hold in the academic discipline of musicology.

Death and Transfiguration

It is often claimed that the tradition of Western classical music is in a state of crisis. But the claim is too sweeping.

It is certainly true that there is a crisis in terms of what is often called 'serious' contemporary music (an unsatisfactory label, obviously, since it implies that music outside the concert-hall tradition cannot be serious), at least if crisis is to be defined in terms of audience statistics. The idea that progressive, new music must by definition be a minority taste—that only an élite will be able to appreciate it—is a historical phenomenon; it goes back to around the beginning of the twentieth century, when there was an explosion of self-consciously 'avant-garde' movements across the arts. The most conspicuous example is painting: reacting against the fossilized conventions of institutionally approved, 'academic' art, young painters developed self-consciously innovative and individualistic styles of work, and published manifestos in which they explained that their work heralded a new artistic movement (Orphism, Vorticism, Futurism, or whatever). And a similar pursuit of innovation spread to the other arts; the Viennese composer Schoenberg, for instance, was extremely self-conscious about the historic significance of his abandonment of tonality (the 'common-practice' system according to which music is organized around a central key or 'tonic'), and his subsequent invention of serialism. He even claimed that it would ensure the dominance of German music for another hundred years (the 'another', of course, is a reference back to Beethoven).

The serial method, which Schoenberg and his followers used from the 1920s, meant constructing music out of the same sequence of notes used over and over again, though it was done in such a way that the results were not as banal or obvious as this makes them sound (so you could use the sequence of notes or 'series' backwards or upside down, you could transpose it up or down so that it began on a different note, and so on). Nevertheless serial music sounded very different from tonal music. Listeners found that many of the familiar musical landmarks had disappeared. And the less the new music sounded like the old, the fewer people listened to it. Those who *did* listen became highly committed to it; modern music became ghettoized as its audiences became increasingly divorced from those who listened to the mainstream classical repertory. But Schoenberg and many of his contemporaries thought that this was merely a transient, if unavoidable, phase: the history of music, they said, showed that audiences always resisted the unfamiliar, but in time they got used to it and learned to appreciate it. (Had not contemporary audiences rejected Beethoven's 'Hammerklavier' Sonata and Ninth Symphony?) Schoenberg himself looked forward to a time when, as he said, grocers' boys would whistle serial music on their rounds.

If Schoenberg really believed what he said (and it is hard to be quite sure about this), then it represents one of the most poignant moments in the history of music. For serialism did not achieve popularity; the process of familiarization for which he and his contemporaries were waiting never occurred. Instead, the label 'modern music' stayed stubbornly attached to the music of a period that passed further and further into history, giving rise to the absurd situation that concert-promoters today may reject as too 'modern' a composition that goes back to the time when our grandparents were children. Why did this happen? Maybe it was because composers like Schoenberg (like Birtwistle) believed too wholeheartedly in the nineteenth-century concept of authenticity, and so treated listeners with something bordering on contempt. (Nineteenth-century composers, by contrast, frequently gave listeners precisely what they wanted, even as they proclaimed the high-minded principles of 'art for art's sake'. The same might be said of progressive rock bands.) Or maybe it was because they believed that lack of popular acclaim guaranteed the seriousness and integrity of their work, and accordingly directed their music to a tiny audience of committed listeners, rather than to the public in general; certainly this is what is suggested by the Society for Private Musical Performances which Schoenberg set up in Vienna in 1918, to whose concerts only bona fide members were admitted, and then on condition that they neither applauded nor allowed any report of the music to appear in the public press. Or perhaps it is just that 'serious' contemporary music was elbowed out by a succession of developments in popular music ('light' music, jazz, rhythm 'n' blues, rock, and so on) that brought other types of contemporary music to unprecedented heights of popularity.

There is a sense, though, in which this rather dismal picture of modern music is misleading. I have presented it as a picture of failure, as if the criterion of success was that the music of Schoenberg, Birtwistle, and the rest should come to occupy the same role in our concert halls, record shops, and sitting-rooms as that of Beethoven and Brahms (or Michael Jackson and The Artist Formerly Known As Prince, for that matter). But there is no reason to assume that they *should* occupy the same slot. I spoke in Chapter 1 of the plurality of subcultures that has replaced the monolithic, institutionally approved culture of nineteenth-century thought. Modern music, or rather 'modern music', flourishes mainly on the fringes of State subsidy and academia, and sometimes also of the entertainment industry (as in soundtracks for horror movies), but the point is that in those areas it *does* flourish. It is a niche product, certainly—but then you could say the same about the Beethoven/Brahms tradition. The difference is just in the size of the niche, and the degree of economic leverage associated with it.

In any case, even if the contemporary wing of the classical tradition is challenged in respect of its client base, so to speak, that is no reason for saying that classical music as a whole is in a state of crisis. To be sure, the tradition has become static, in the sense that its centre of gravity does not keep pace with the passing of time; if a few modern masterpieces join the classical repertory each decade, they are counterbalanced by the extension of the repertory backwards into the Renaissance and medieval periods—the field of so-called 'early music'. But this might be more logically presented as a growth than a decline of the tradition. And the development and dissemination of sound reproduction technology means that, on any conceivable statistical measure, classical music reaches an exponentially greater audience across the world than has ever previously been the case. What is more, it is heard in performances of a quality altogether unattainable by provincial orchestras of the nineteenth century, and perhaps even by those of the capitals; a major reason for such problems as early audiences may have had with such seminal works as the Ninth Symphony, Berlioz's *Symphonie fantastique*, and Stravinsky's *Rite of Spring* was almost certainly that they were played by under-rehearsed, underpaid, and probably puzzled musicians. Since sound recording had not been invented, however, we shall never know for sure.

It would be easy to go on in this vein. Within the last decade, for instance,

- the studiously unkempt violinist now known as Kennedy (aka The Artist Formerly Known as Nigel) released a video of Vivaldi's *The Four Seasons*, bringing pop promotion techniques to the classical repertory; he should

probably be held personally responsible for its ubiquitous use today in telephone systems the world over. (How
often have you had to listen to a tinny-sounding rendition
of *The Four Seasons* while on hold?)

- the three tenors—Luciano Pavarotti, Placido Domingo,
  and José Carreras—brought Italian opera into the pop
  charts following the adoption of their recording of
  Puccini's aria 'Nessun dorma' as the official anthem of
  the World Cup.
- the Third Symphony of the hitherto almost unheard-of
  Polish composer Henryk Górecki nudged Madonna out
  of the charts after being heavily plugged by Classic FM,
  the London-based classical music station.
- the pianist David Helfgott shot into public prominence
  following the release of *Shine*, a film that traced his long
  fight against mental illness; audiences flocked to his
  performances of the classics, though the critics panned
  them.

But it is not really necessary to cite such exceptional cases
in order to show how the music industry has successfully
repositioned classical music as a largely profitable niche
product—a *major* niche product—in contemporary consumer culture.

And for this reason it seems to me that rumours of the death
of classical music have been greatly exaggerated. Lawrence
Kramer, for instance, writes that

It is no secret that, in the United States anyway, this music is in
trouble. It barely registers in our schools, it has neither the pres-
tige nor the popularity of literature and visual art, and it squan-
ders its capacities for self-renewal by clinging to an exceptionally
static core repertoire. Its audience is shrinking, graying, and
overly pale-faced, and the suspicion has been voiced abroad that
its claim to occupy a sphere of autonomous artistic greatness is
largely a means of veiling, and thus perpetuating, a narrow set of
social interests.

And Kramer is by no means the only commentator to express such fears; in 1996 the opera director Peter Sellars even likened classical music to 'a cancer patient or an AIDS patient'. All the same, I think that the diagnosis is not quite accurate. Classical music is not dead, probably not even dying, and certainly not in Europe; GCSE and the National Curriculum have maintained the presence of classical music in British classrooms, and I have already referred to the classical music magazines that have proliferated on news-stand shelves since around the time Classic FM began broadcasting. But what has kept it alive is a dramatic transformation of its social and cultural role—a transformation epitomized by Classic FM, whose practice of excerpting single movements from classical symphonies outraged highbrow critics. The problem is that this transformation has been barely acknowledged in academic (and not-so-academic) writing about music, much of which still attempts to sustain an image of classical music—indeed an image of music in general—that is now beyond resuscitation.

In other words, if there is a crisis in classical music, it is not in the music itself, but in ways of *thinking* about it—and it is these ways of thinking about music that form the central topic of this book. In particular, there are two habits of thought which are deeply ingrained in Western culture as a whole and which largely determine the way we traditionally think about music. One might be called the tendency to explain away time; it is this that leads us to think of music as a kind of imaginary object, something (and the word 'thing' is significant in this context) which is *in* time but not *of* time. The other is the tendency to think of language and other forms of cultural representation, including music, as if they depicted some kind of external reality. I have mentioned each of these in passing but they need explaining and illustrating at greater length, and so they form the topics of the next two chapters.

And yet, and yet . . . there *are* times when music of the classical symphonic tradition does not quite ring true to me. Increasingly it seems to me that there is something a bit forced . . . Isn't there perhaps something a bit forced about Brahms's symphonies, say—at one moment too noisily bombastic with their parade-ground rhythms, and at the next moment too self-indulgently sentimental. I don't notice it so much with piano or chamber music (or opera, for that matter); the problem lies with the public, sometimes tub-thumping, always self-conscious genre of the symphony. I still admire the music as much as ever. But I used to just love it, and that's the difference. Is it that the music is aging badly, as Kramer fears? Is it because I'm hearing it increasingly critically, in the sense that I describe in later chapters of this book—as something that isn't just 'natural' but brings with it the no longer credible values of a defunct society? (Could this have something to do with the stereotypically gendered construction of the public sphere in the nineteenth century? That would link with the ideas I present in Chapter 7.) Then again, is it because in these days of public-sector stringency the need for all those dinner-jacketed musicians seems too wilfully extravagant, by comparison to the lean efficiency and flexibility of today's pop groups, or early music groups for that matter? (A lot of people find the subsidized extravagance of the opera house offensive.) Or does it just come from seeing the music on television, where those intrusive close-ups of the musicians crowd out the music's own values (why else do we speak of 'seeing' it?), reduplicating what is already in the sound and so rendering it banal? I don't know, and I find it a bit unsettling.

4 An Imaginary Object

Stopping Time in its Tracks

Ronald Searle's cartoon (Fig. 13), a scene from the apocryphal English girls' school St Trinian's, turns on the curious presence that music has in our lives and our thoughts. It is there, and yet it isn't. Or more precisely signs of it are everywhere—in scores, books, instruments—and yet they aren't the music. You can't point to the music, or grasp hold of it, because as soon as it has come into being it has already disappeared, swallowed up into silence, leaving no trace. Only at St Trinian's do you get to sweep up the debris.

And what are the crotchets and quavers that the cleaning women have to contend with (or quarters and eighth-notes, as they would be if St Trinian's were in America)? What are they for, what work do they do within our musical culture? You might say that they serve three distinct functions. One, the most obvious, is *conservation*: like photographs, they stop time in its tracks and give a stable, visible form to the evanescent. The second is almost equally obvious: they are a means for the *communication* of music from one person to another, for example (but it is only an example) from composer to performer. The third is less obvious but at least as important as the other two: notation is integral to the *conception* of music, to the ways in which composers, performers, and all others who work with music imagine or think about it.

'Ruddy music lessons...'

Fig. 13. Cartoon by Ronald Searle

Many ancient civilizations, most notoriously that of Egypt, seem to have been haunted by a dread of decay and forgetfulness, and so attempted almost obsessively to give a permanent form to everything that their civilization embraced, to fix it for eternity; hence the existence of such time capsules as Tutankhamun's tomb. Many cultures have been possessed by a similar desire to give music a tangible, enduring presence, and so the music of vanished societies survives to this day in the precarious form of fragile manuscripts in Japanese temples, European monastic archives, and American libraries ('precarious' because much of this music survives in only a single exemplar. It is a striking fact that all the extant sources for the 'polyphonic' or multi-part music of the medieval period—the kind of music that is played by 'early music' groups—could if brought together be piled up on a single, fairly large dining-table.)

But 'survive' is perhaps too strong a word, for the music of the past exists in a kind of half-life. Even if you understand how a notation works (and it took years of patient scholarly work to decode some of the notations used for early medieval music, while the interpretation of others remains contentious), there are aspects of the music about which the notation is silent. Medieval chant, for instance, survives in a variety of 'neumatic' notations, essentially consisting of symbols showing whether groups of notes go up, or down, or up a bit and then down, and so on (Fig. 14). But how fast are you meant to sing the music, and what sort of vocal production did the monks who sang it employ? Did they project their voices loudly, or sing softly, or nasally, or gutturally? With or without vibrato? The notation does not say and nobody knows.

The same problems apply to far more recent music, too. You might assume that we would know how a nineteenth-century composition like Gounod's Ave Maria, say, was performed in its own time; after all, it has enjoyed a continuous

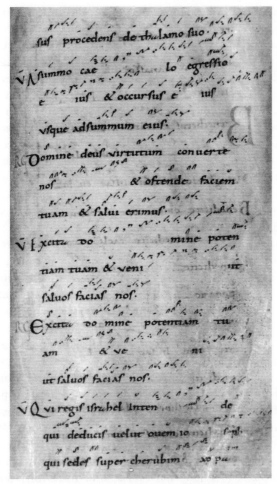

Fig. 14. Cantatorium of St Gall (Stiftsbibliothek St Gallen, Cod. 359), p. 31. Early neumes, written above the words and looking more or less like an *aide-mémoire*, summarize the shape of the melody but do not specify the exact intervals; it is impossible to transcribe them into modern notation without guesswork. This manuscript dates from the late ninth century

performance tradition, unlike earlier music that has had to be laboriously reconstructed from the original sources. But there is a very early recording, dating from 1904, which casts doubt on this. It was made by Alessandro Moreschi, the last castrato, who was in his time called 'the angel of Rome'. During the seventeenth and eighteenth centuries boys with especially promising voices were sometimes castrated to prevent their voices breaking, and the resulting male sopranos took the lead roles in opera as well as singing in choirs, such as that of the Sistine Chapel; Moreschi was himself a member, and from 1898 the conductor, of the Sistine Chapel Choir. But the practice was increasingly seen as barbaric and died out in the nineteenth century, so that Moreschi (born as late as 1858) represents the very end of the tradition.

And behind the hiss and crackle you can hear a rendition of the Ave Maria that sounds extraordinary to modern ears. There are specific features you might pick out; for instance, Moreschi glides rapidly on to some of the notes from an octave or more below, in a way that no modern singer would. But it is the *sound* of his voice, what you might call the tonal ideal embodied in it, that seems most bizarre: it has an acute, almost painful focus, as if it were a kind of sublimated primal scream. Of course we don't know whether the recording exemplified Moreschi at his best; he may well have been nervous, for early recording processes were very intrusive. And we don't know how far the way Moreschi sung the Ave Maria is typical of how it was sung elsewhere. Maybe the recording sounded as strange to Moreschi's contemporaries as it does to us. But then again, maybe it did not. And that is the point: we don't know, and what is more there is no way we ever can know. The conclusion is obvious: if we don't really know what music sounded like at the turn of the twentieth century, how can we possibly know what medieval music sounded like? The honest answer is that we can't.

Notation conserves music, then, but it conceals as much as it reveals. At the same time, and largely through its particular pattern of concealment and revelation, notation plays a central role in the maintenance and even the definition of musical culture. To see how this may be, however, we need to go into a little more detail about what musical notations are and how they work. And right at the beginning we need to distinguish two different types of notation, or more precisely two ways in which notations can work: by representing sounds, and by representing things that performers have to do in order to make sounds. Although musical notations often combine them, these are quite different principles.

The standard Western staff notation—to which the crotchets and quavers of Ronald Searle's cartoon belong—basically works by representing sounds, just like the neumatic notation for medieval chant which I mentioned above. (That is not surprising, since the one evolved from the other.) So each notehead represents a separate note, and how high or low the note is depends on how high or low on the page the notehead is. The horizontal lines that make up the staff, against which the noteheads are placed, are there to provide easy reference; they evolved by stages, reaching their modern form by around 1200. And of course the passage of time is represented by the left–right axis of the page. In principle, then, modern Western notation is a kind of two-dimensional picture of the music, letting you see how it goes at a glance.

I say 'in principle' because in practice it isn't so simple. For one thing, there are various symbolic elements in the notation—elements whose meaning is fixed by convention, and that you couldn't guess if you didn't know the convention. (Examples include the different types of notehead and beam used to represent the duration of a note, and the arbitrarily shaped signs that indicate rests.) Then again, there are elements that don't represent the sound in any direct way, but that represent something you should do to make the sound—in other words, that correspond to the second notational principle I mentioned. An example is when you see 'una corda' in a piece of piano music: it means that you should press the right-hand pedal, which shifts the hammers sideways so that they only strike one string (in Italian, *una corda*) instead of the usual two or three, resulting in a thinner, more translucent sound. As I said, then, 'una corda' doesn't describe the sound but what you do to make the sound, and this is the principle that defines the type of notation known as 'tablature'.

There are many different examples of tablature notation. Some are found in the West, for instance the tablatures used during the Renaissance for guitar and lute music, or the modern guitar-symbol notation found in popular sheet music. The point about guitar-symbol notation is that it is much easier to learn than staff notation; instead of showing you how the music is meant to sound and leaving you to translate that into whatever you have to do to make the sound on your particular instrument, it simply tells you where to put your fingers on the guitar fingerboard. In a sense, you don't have to understand what the notation is saying, you just *do* it. Of course, guitar-symbol notation is much more limited than staff notation; you can't use it to notate tunes, only chords (but that is not a problem since it is generally used alongside staff notation for the tune), and even then it doesn't tell you whether to play the chord once, or strum it regularly, or in a particular rhythm. That is up to you.

But the real limitation of tablatures, if it is fair to call it a limitation, is a different one. Unlike Western staff notation, whose generality makes it more or less applicable to any instrument, each tablature only works for one instrument, because the things you have to do to play a particular tune, say, vary from one instrument to another. And in cultures where every instrument has its own tablature, the result is that there is little sense of an overall, unified musical tradition that embraces them all; in this sense it makes less sense to talk of 'traditional Chinese music' than to talk of *qin* music, *yangqin* music, *pipa* music, and so on (all of these are different types of plucked or hammered string instruments). In the West, by contrast, we have far more of a sense that there is a coherent tradition called 'Western music' which reaches both back in time and, nowadays, across the globe, and this sense is rooted in our almost universal acceptance of the system of staff notation. (For us, tablatures are mainly associated with instruments designed for amateurs, such as the now more or less obsolete autoharp, which you strummed with one hand while pressing down a bar with the other. The bar automatically selected the correct strings for the chord you wanted to play.) Small wonder, then, that when children start having piano or clarinet or violin lessons they find themselves—sometimes to their chagrin—spending a lot of time away from their instruments, studying what, in an extremely odd use of the term, is known as 'theory'. What they are basically acquiring is a knowledge of notation, and through it an initiation into the culture of Western music.

And it is this, far more than any aesthetic considerations of 'high' or 'low' art, that makes it hard to be sure whether we should think of jazz, rock, and pop as all part of the same tradition as 'classical' music, or whether they should really be thought of as separate traditions; after all, many jazz, rock, and pop musicians don't read music. On the other hand plenty do, and sheet-music sales of popular music show how readily this music can be accommodated within the framework of staff notation. And more and more there are musicians who move effortlessly between one tradition and another. It seems both that there is and there isn't such a thing as 'Western music'.

Music between the Notes

DAT recorders and samplers are entirely unselective, in the sense that within global limits of fidelity they will record *anything*. In this they are quite unlike musical notations and, more generally, any of the systems that different cultures employ for representing musical sounds (including, for instance, the spoken syllables used by Indian tabla players to memorize complex rhythmic patterns and the conventionalized gestures of Western conductors, as well as the graphic notations with which this chapter is primarily concerned). For musical notations are highly specific about what they will or will not record; they are more like filters or prisms than DAT recorders or samplers. And ethnomusicologists, who use essentially Western techniques to study non-Western music, are more aware of this than anyone.

Some ethnomusicologists are prepared to use staff notation to transcribe the music they study, as a means both of understanding it and of communicating that understanding to their readers. But they are painfully conscious that in doing this they are shoehorning Indian or Chinese music, or whatever it might be, into a system that was never designed for it. For instance, staff notation treats all music as if it were made up of separate notes each a set distance apart; in effect it assumes that all instruments work on the same principle as the piano, which has a separate sound-producing mechanism for each of the eighty-eight notes it can play. But many instruments are not like this; on the violin you can play any number of pitches between a B and a C, say, or you can slide continuously from the one note to the other so that there is no way in which you can say exactly where the B ended and the C started. The same applies to the human voice, or the electric guitar if you use the vibrato arm. And the point is that in Indian and Chinese music it is often the notes between the notes, so to speak, that are responsible for the effect of the music. Similarly in florid singing (and again Indian music is a good example) trying to say where one note starts and another stops, as 'note' would be defined in terms of staff notation, becomes a completely arbitrary exercise; the music just doesn't work that way. There is a collision between music and notation.

Predictably, this situation has resulted in endless contro-

versies between those ethnomusicologists who see staff notation as a blunt but necessary instrument for conveying something of the music to readers unfamiliar with the notational
system (if any) of the musical culture in question, and those
who regard its use as a kind of neo-colonial exercise in which
Western notation is set up as a universal standard. But to put
it like this makes it sound as if there is a choice between black
and white, whereas it is really a matter of shades of grey. For
if staff notation distorts non-Western music, you might just as
well argue that it distorts the music of the Western tradition
too. You only have to listen to a synthesized performance of
Chopin's E minor Prelude, in which every note is equally long
and equally loud, to realize how much of the music's effect lies
in the shaping of time and dynamics that any pianist brings to
the music, quite possibly without even thinking about it
(though some pianists do it better than others, of course, and
that is a major part of what being a good pianist means). It's
not that the synthesizer's performance is wrong, in the sense
of contradicting the score; the temporal and dynamic shaping
isn't in the score. And that says something about what scores
are and how they are used.

If we treated notation the way some Christian fundamen-
talists treat the Bible—if we said that anything that isn't in the
score shouldn't be in the performance—then computer-
controlled synthesizers would by now have put performers
out of a job: it takes a machine to perform the music literally,
mindlessly, without expression. But we don't treat notation
this way. The fact that the notation doesn't care about
subtleties of temporal or dynamic shaping doesn't mean *we*
don't care about them. And if our notation simplifies the music
by eliminating these things, that is because it is in the nature
of notations to simplify. A notation that tried to put *everything*
in would end up being far too complicated to read. (Again
ethnomusicologists have experience of this; Charles Seeger,
the pioneer of North American ethnomusicology, invented
the melograph, a device that transcribed every smallest

nuance of timing, dynamics, and pitch, but the resulting graphs are so complex that nobody has ever really figured out what to do with them.) All notations miss things out, then, only different things. You can see this from the history of Western 'art' music. Eighteenth-century composers sometimes wrote down just the skeleton of what they intended, leaving the performer to flesh it out through figuration and ornamentation; twentieth-century composers, by contrast, generally try to specify what they want in far more detail. But even in the most extreme cases, such as the piano music of Pierre Boulez or Karlheinz Stockhausen, there is still room for variation—as you can tell from the fact that their music sounds different when different pianists play it (not that very many do).

But the best way to make this point is by comparing the different notations in use across the world. The tablature used for the Chinese long zither or *qin*, traditionally the instrument of choice for scholars and gentlemen (Fig. 15), is a good example. It states in some detail how each note is to be produced (with the fleshy part of the finger or the nail, with an inward or outward motion, and so on), all of which adds up to a precise specification of the note's tone-quality, or timbre. By contrast, and despite its unparalleled overall complexity and comprehensiveness, staff notation has difficulty saying anything about timbre, other than specifying what instrument the music is for. But there are other respects in which *qin* notation is far less specific than staff notation. In particular, it doesn't specify rhythm; it just represents the music as a chain of notes (or more precisely, a sequence of gestures), leaving it up to the performer to decide what notes to play faster and slower, whether and how to group them together into phrases, and so forth. That doesn't mean the Chinese don't care about these things, any more than Western listeners don't care about violin timbre. On the contrary, there are whole schools of *qin* performance based on different ways of performing the *qin* repertory. It is just like the different tradi-

Fig. 15. Za Fuxi (1895–1976), scholar and performer on the *qin*

tions of piano playing that bring different qualities to the performance of the repertory, even though each of them involves playing the same notes. It would not be that much of an exaggeration to say that the whole art of performance lies in the interstices of notation, in those parts of the music that the score cannot reach.

I said that the most obvious function of notation was conservation. If that were its only function, then the development of digital sound recording would have rendered traditional notation obsolete; in terms of comprehensiveness and fidelity, no other means of representing music can possibly compare with a CD (except a vinyl record, according to some audio buffs, but I am not going to enter into that controversy). The fact that we go on using traditional notation, then, demonstrates the importance to us of its other functions. For through the process of communicating information from composer to performer, or more generally from one musician to another, notations at the same time do something much more complex: they transmit a whole way of thinking about music. A score sets up a framework that identifies certain attributes of the music as essential, in the sense that if your performance doesn't have those attributes then you can't really claim to have been performing that music at all. If you play the E minor Prelude and get one note wrong, then nobody (except one or two philosophers) will claim that what you played wasn't the E minor Prelude. But heaven knows what they will say if you get 95 per cent of the notes wrong. Somewhere between these limits lies the essential note-to-note structure that identifies the E minor Prelude.

But the essential note-to-note structure is only part of the music. For between and around these notes, so to speak, lies a vast domain of interpretive possibility, in which you can choose to play faster or slower, louder or softer, to phrase or articulate one way or another. None of this impinges on whether or not you can claim to be playing the E minor Prelude. Rather, it is what makes your performance individualistic, drab, eccentric, emotionally self-indulgent, or just plain brilliant.

Master of the Smallest Link

The pattern of what is determined by notation and what isn't, what is to be taken as given and what is a matter of performance interpretation, is one of the things that defines a musical culture; it defines not only how music is transmitted but also how the various individuals whose activities together make up a musical culture relate to one another. It also largely determines how people imagine music within a given culture—most obviously how composers conceive their music, though you could say that it is shared patterns of imagination that bind *all* the members of a musical community together. To compose within any given tradition, then, is to imagine sounds in terms of the particular configurations of determinacy and indeterminacy appropriate to that tradition, and this in turns means that notation is much more profoundly implicated in the act of composition than many accounts of the compositional process might lead you to believe.

There are two famous sources relating to the ways in which Mozart and Beethoven respectively conceived their music. In a letter that only came to light at the beginning of the nineteenth century (it was first published in 1815), Mozart explained how musical ideas would come to him unbidden, and enlarge themselves in his mind until

the whole, though it be long, stands almost finished and complete in my mind, so that I can survey it, like a fine picture or a beautiful statue, at a glance. . . . [T]he committing to paper is done quickly enough, for every thing is . . . already finished; and it rarely differs on paper, from what it was in my imagination.

And corroboration of this account of the compositional process comes from the composer Louis Schlösser, who at the age of 85 published an account of a meeting he had with Beethoven more than sixty years before, in 1822. Schlösser paraphrased Beethoven's words:

I carry my thoughts about me for a long time, often a very long time, before I write them down. . . . I change many things, discard and try again until I am satisfied. . . . [I]n so much as I know exactly what I want, the fundamental idea never deserts me—it arises before me, grows—I see and hear the picture in all its extent and dimensions stand before my mind like a cast and there remains for me nothing but the labor of writing it down, which is quickly accomplished.

The degree of consensus between these accounts is remarkable. Both Mozart and Beethoven emphasize how they can 'see' or 'survey' the music at a glance, and compare it to a picture (even Beethoven's reference to it as a cast chimes in with Mozart's 'statue'). And both insist that the real work of composition is done in the mind, with writing it down being a trivial matter. Notation, as they describe it, is not something integral to the creative process at all; it comes strictly after the event.

Both these accounts harmonize perfectly with the way of thinking about music which I described in Chapter 2. Mozart and Beethoven are telling us that the conception of music is a purely ideal process, an achievement of the imagination un-trammelled by the mechanical process of setting pen to paper. They give us a perfect image of the inspired composer, the 'master of the smallest link' (to borrow a phrase from Theodor Adorno) whose vision—a term whose biblical resonances are entirely pertinent—encompasses every detail of the music's unfolding. This is an image of authorship that borders on the divine; indeed it echoes theological accounts of the moment of Creation, in which God envisages every tiniest ramification of what He has created. For Mozart and Beethoven, as for God, creation is focused on what might be called a moment of truth into which all temporal unfolding is compressed, and it is this moment of truth that editors, performers, musicolo-gists, and critics all try in their different ways to recapture. It is hardly surprising, then, that these stirring accounts of the compositional process were quoted and requoted by count-less musicians of the nineteenth and early twentieth centuries (for example, they feature prominently in Schenker's final book, *Der freie Satz*). And what makes all this doubly remark-able is the striking contrast between what Beethoven said, as transmitted by Schlösser, and what we know of the externals of his compositional process.

For Beethoven took scraps of paper, and later pocket-sized sketchbooks, with him on his frequent walks in the country-side near Vienna, instantly jotting down his musical ideas in case he forgot them; at home, he kept larger sketchbooks on his desk into which he might copy the results or enter new ideas, fashioning and refashioning the music, developing it bit by bit, correcting or adding to it, crossing it out and start-ing again. After Beethoven's death these sketchbooks were dispersed and in many cases broken up, but one of the most sustained research programmes in postwar musicology has succeeded in reconstructing their original sequence. As a result, you can work through them and trace the laborious and sometimes almost painful process by which Beethoven edged (sometimes directly and sometimes via enormous detours) towards the music that we know. For instance, while the first section of the 'Ode to Joy' seems to have come to him with little difficulty, the middle section gave him enormous trouble; there is sketch upon sketch in which Beethoven tries one idea, then another, sometimes working out different options systematically and sometimes apparently taking pot-shots at random. And again and again you find that the most characteristic and expressive features of the music come together only during the final stages of the compositional process; as Gustav Nottebohm (the first serious scholar of Beethoven's sketchbooks) put it, 'in most humans the creative faculty grows slack with work, but with Beethoven it was otherwise, for in him it worked on unimpaired: indeed it often rose to its greatest heights only at the last moment'.

The explanation for the striking disparity between what Beethoven said and what he did is in fact depressingly simple, and the story has been told by Maynard Solomon. The letter attributed to Mozart was almost certainly an invention of Friedrich Rochlitz, the journalist and critic who edited the magazine in which it first appeared. And Schlösser's account of his conversation with Beethoven was almost certainly copied consciously or unconsciously from Rochlitz's letter; the two are just too similar for any other interpretation to be plausible. Contemporaries believed these accounts were authentic not because they corresponded to how Mozart or Beethoven composed (this is obvious at least in the case of Beethoven), nor even probably because they corresponded to what Mozart or Beethoven said (remember each account appeared long after the composer's death), but because they represented what, in nineteenth-century eyes, the composers *ought* to have said. In short, they tell us a great deal about the thinking of the Romantic period, but little about Mozart, Beethoven, or the compositional process.

If we put these exercises in myth-making to one side, we can see just how far the way in which Beethoven conceived music was tied up with the way in which he notated it. The frenzies of writing, rewriting, crossing-out, and redrafting to which sketches like Fig. 16 bear evidence do not record Beethoven's advance towards the preordained 'fundamental idea' that, in Schlösser's words, never deserted him. On the contrary, they show the music being forged, hammered so to speak on the anvil of pen and paper. This is no disembodied process; sometimes, as you pore over the sketchbooks, you have an almost visceral sense of Beethoven's pen digging into the fibrous, handmade paper as he struggled to give expression to some recalcitrant, half-formed idea. At other times you can sense the music emerging from the page as Beethoven literally *saw* what he meant. When we talk about Beethoven 'writing' a symphony, then, there is nothing metaphorical about such language; we are talking about a physical engagement of pen and paper, and about a creative act that was inseparable from the imperatives and resistances of Western staff notation.

We know so much about Beethoven's compositional process because of the peculiar way he composed (sketched, doodled, calculated, improvised) on paper, and this is a personal trait that started long before he became deaf; if he had not worked this way, it seems unlikely that he could have gone on composing as he did after his deafness had become profound. But most classical composers did not compose like this; that means we know less about how they composed, and it also means that it is dangerous to generalize from what Beethoven did to what other composers did. But it seems unlikely that any composers just sat there until they were full of music, and then poured it all on to the page. (According to contemporary accounts Mozart and Schubert came closest to this, but even they sketched, corrected, and recorrected their

Fig. 16. Autograph of Beethoven's unfinished piano concerto, Hess 15 (Staatsbibliothek zu Berlin, MS Artaria 184), p. 18. This half-completed score uses an old-fashioned layout in which the top three staves show the violins and violas, while the fourth stave from the bottom shows the cellos and basses

music on paper.) For classical composers had another device for grappling with the representation of music, trying things out, shaping them against empirical resistance—and this was a device that did not leave visible traces like Beethoven's sketches (or the St Trinian's music lessons). This device was the piano.

You will sometimes hear the view expressed that real composers compose at their desks, not at the keyboard. (The practice of public examinations in harmony and counterpoint seems to be based on this idea, since otherwise it would hardly make sense to lock students away in examination rooms and expect them to come out with music.) And there have been composers who could do this. There is a story of the French composer Maurice Ravel coming into Vaughan Williams's study one day, and finding the Englishman working away at his desk. Ravel was horror-stricken; 'how can you find new chords without a piano?', he asked. And the incensed, hugely frustrated letters in which composers like Chopin and Mahler railed against inefficient piano-dealers who failed to deliver instruments on time and so prevented them from getting on with their work show that there were other composers, too, who would have sided with Ravel. (It is fortunate that Chopin, Mahler, and Ravel did not have to compose in an examination room.) The idea that there is something wrong with composing at the keyboard is just another example of the nineteenth-century myth that music is something pure and disembodied, coming unbidden from the spirit realm. Composers know that music is not something that just happens, like the weather. It is something you make.

The Paradox of Music

In 1973–4 the avant-garde composer György Ligeti, who was born in Hungary but came over to the West after the Russian invasion in 1956, composed an orchestral piece called *San Francisco Polyphony*. Like much of Ligeti's music around that time, it is a densely written piece, a jungle of sinuous, creeper-like melodic lines. But Ligeti used a different metaphor to explain how he had tried to contain the sometimes impenetrable note-to-note patterning of the music within orderly bounds: 'One can imagine various objects in a state of total disarray in a drawer,' he wrote. 'The drawer too has a definite form. Inside it chaos reigns, but it is clearly defined itself.' A metaphor like this captures certain salient aspects of the music, while saying nothing about others; for this reason there are other pieces of music it might apply to just as well, and equally there are other metaphors that might apply just as well to *San Francisco Polyphony*. If the music strikes you as just an impenetrable tangle of sound, then listening to it with Ligeti's drawer image in mind may provide a way into it. Or to use my alternative metaphor, once you know the extent of the forest, you may find it easier to discern faint paths through the undergrowth.

We don't usually think of music in the form of drawers or forests and so these metaphors stand out as imaginative representations of it—imaginative representations that, at best, can in some way add to or empower our experience of the music. (A good deal of critical writing about music consists in essence of developing illuminating metaphors to describe individual compositions; in the nineteenth century this approach acquired the biblically inspired term 'hermeneutics', implying that it sought out the meaning behind the music.) But all descriptions of music involve metaphor; it is just that the metaphor is not always so obvious. To see that this is so, just try to talk about music without falling into metaphor. One of the most basic things you might want to say is that one note is higher and lower than another. But that doesn't mean that high notes literally come from the sky and low ones from abysmal, subterranean depths (though it might seem that way if you listen respectively to Vaughan Williams's *The Lark Ascending* and Wagner's *Rheingold Prelude*). It is just a metaphor: somehow high notes are more compact, brighter, lighter, higher . . . and of course in staff notation they appear higher on the page. Then again, you might talk about the texture of a piece of music. Texture? Bark, moss, velvet, sacking: these things have texture, but how can music have texture when you can't touch it? And what did you mean when you referred to a 'piece' of music? Do you tear strips of music off a roll, like cloth, or chip them off a block? A block of what?

Metaphor is built into our language, and so deeply that we usually don't even notice it is there. And along with the metaphors of music being a drawer or a forest, these embedded metaphors all illustrate what might be called the underlying, root metaphor of Western musical culture: that music is some kind of object. Mozart and Beethoven, or rather Rochlitz and Schlösser, expressed this very clearly when they spoke of it as a painting or statue. But the metaphor of music as object goes much deeper than the myth-making process of nineteenth-century musical aesthetics; you simply can't get away from it, unless you are prepared to stop talking about music altogether (and people will never stop talking about something they care about as much as music). The whole idea of writing music depends on it: Western staff notation shows music 'moving' up and down and from left to right on the page. But what is it that actually does the moving? Literally, nothing; as Roger Scruton has made clear, when we say the music moves, we are treating it as an imaginary object. The same applies when you flick back in a score, comparing two passages of the music side by side. After all, you can't fold time like paper; when you compare the earlier passage with the later one, you are in effect peeling the music away from the passage of time and so transforming a temporal experience into an imaginary object. That is one of the things that scores are for.

And here is the basic paradox of music. We experience it in time but in order to manipulate it, even to understand it, we pull it out of time and in that sense falsify it. But it isn't a falsification we can do without; it is a basic part of what music *is* (and not just Western art music, I would claim, since *all* musical cultures are built on representation, whether notational, gestural, or otherwise. However, I won't argue the point). The important thing is to recognize the falsification for what it is, and not to confuse the imaginary objects of music with the temporal experiences for which they stand. There is a widespread, and perhaps partly justified, view that this is one of the problems that beset new music after the Second World War, when 'serious' composition became the preserve of university music departments; certain composers intellectualized more and more about what went into the score, almost as if they were constructing mathematical proofs in sound, apparently oblivious to the fact that none of this was conveyed to their diminishing audiences. But the confusion of imaginary object and experience is ineradicable. When you go to a shop and say 'Have you got any music by Sorabji?' you are asking whether they have the score or CD that you want; as I said at the beginning of this chapter, the *music* is something else. (And remember how Piginini, who could only play with 'the music' in front of him, had to be taught how to play *music*.) As is so often the case when we talk about music, we don't quite say what we mean, or mean what we say. Or to put it another way, whenever we try to talk about music, we seem to end up changing the subject.

So where does that leave the imaginary museum that I described in Chapter 2, that Tutankhamun's tomb of the most complex and considered of imaginary objects, musical works? Isn't the whole idea of the imaginary museum built on a confusion of imaginary objects and temporal experiences? I can think of two answers to this, one radical, and one less so. The less radical answer is to say that if musical works are not experiences but merely their surrogates, so to speak, then the same might be said of the contents of any other museum: paintings, for instance, are bought and sold (and insured and stolen) as physical objects, but we go to the gallery to look at them not for themselves, but for the experiences we can derive from them—and there are as many ways in which they can be experienced as there are people experiencing them. I shall explore some of the ramifications of that idea in the next chapter.

The more radical answer (or perhaps it is just the same answer expressed more radically) is suggested by the biologist Richard Dawkins's profoundly unsettling image of the 'river of genes'. We think of human history, and the prehistoric development of our species, as made up of a vast succession of individual people; as they have bred and interbred, so genes have passed between them, flowing from generation to generation and determining the ethnic, physical, and mental make-up of the human race today. But Dawkins turns this upside down. He makes the genes the protagonists of the story, the true creators of history, with their only motive (if so anthropomorphic a word can properly be used of genes) being one of replication. In this version of the story, humans are reduced to temporary constellations of genes, mere eddies in the river of life. And maybe we should see the contents of the musical museum the same way. For music history has traditionally been presented rather in the manner of a series of stepping-stones, a journey from one masterwork to another, leading from the remote past to the present and beyond. (Old-fashioned music appreciation texts are full of terms like the 'course' of history or the 'procession' of great composers.) Or to use a more appropriate metaphor, perhaps, it is presented as a kind of museum tour, in which you pause to admire each imaginary object before moving on to the next.

On the Dawkins model, it would all be the other way round. The historical process would reside not in musical works—the stepping-stones—but in what lies between them: the continuously changing (as well as geographically variable) patterns of conception and perception which brought those works into being. We would see musical works as the mere traces of historical processes, empty shells into which life can be breathed only through an imaginative reconstruction of the musical experiences that once gave them meaning. And the imagination that is involved in this is our own; you might almost say that we would see the history of music as, in essence, an account of our own journey through the imaginary museum of musical works. Again, then, we come back to the idea that when we study music, we aren't just studying something separate from us, something 'out there': there is a sense in which we are studying ourselves, too.

It could hardly be otherwise, if music is an imaginary object.

5 A Matter of Representation

Two Models of Art

The philosopher Ludwig Wittgenstein once compared understanding a sentence to understanding a musical theme. He did this in the course of an argument against what he called the 'picture' theory of meaning. By this he meant the idea, which I briefly mentioned in Chapter 1, that language represents an external reality existing independently of language—that language is only a medium, in other words. His point was that, whereas you might plausibly regard a sentence like 'John is hitting Mary' as simply a representation of a fact that in itself has nothing to do with language, you can't think of a musical theme that way: to understand a musical theme is simply to understand that musical theme, not to understand some external reality that the musical theme represents.

But the 'picture' theory of meaning is deeply embedded in Western culture, and what might be called 'classical' aesthetics—basically deriving from Plato with a generous admixture of eighteenth-century thought—is in essence an attempt to apply the 'picture' theory to the arts. The visual arts are the most obvious example. If the point of painting or sculpture is to picture the appearance of things as they really are—and even more if it is to picture them as they ideally should be, for instance as in Michelangelo's representation of the human body in *David*—then there are absolute standards by which art can be judged. And these standards have nothing to do with the circumstances that brought it into being or the reasons why it was produced; they relate only to the work of art itself. In fact it becomes the hallmark of true art that it transcends social or historical context and embodies eternal values. It follows from this that art must be appreciated and enjoyed for itself, in an act of almost religious contemplation. In this way classical aesthetics created the image of the autonomous connoisseur or critic, someone who is detached from the processes of artistic creation but who upholds and applies timeless standards of artistic truth and beauty.

The idea of the timeless, quasi-religious work of art ties in with nineteenth-century thinking about music. But music was brought within the framework of classical aesthetics well before that. I have already described, and illustrated, one of the ways in which music was seen as an imitation of something that lies outside music: the idea, going back at least as far as Pythagoras, that music is a representation of cosmic harmony, a microcosmic representation of the macrocosm. Picturesque or whimsical as this idea may seem today, it persisted throughout the Middle Ages and the Renaissance. By the eighteenth century, however, it had been supplanted by another and more flexible idea of musical imitation, known as the theory of affects. 'Affect', in this context, means something halfway between 'mood' and 'passion', and according to this theory music derived its meaning from its ability to capture and convey such affects as love, rage, or jealousy. Seen this way, music's full potential was realized on the operatic stage, where it provided the emotional backdrop to the dramatic words and actions (and you can see how, from this point of view, 'pure' music—music without words—was seen as a poor relation, at best a truncated version of the real thing). Music had meaning, in short, because it represented a reality outside music.

So the history of music doesn't entirely support Wittgenstein's assumption that you can't think of a musical theme as a representation of something else. Wittgenstein's point, however, was that there is an alternative way to see meaning, whether in music or language. His central argument was that, as I put it in Chapter 1, language constructs reality rather than merely reflecting it. It is easy to show that language *can* work like this. If you promise something, your words are not a verbal report of something that took place elsewhere; the words *are* the promise. (It makes no sense to say 'I promised my husband I would be faithful to him in future, but did not tell him until the following morning.') In other words, in saying 'I promise' you are *doing* something, not just reporting on something. What Wittgenstein was suggesting was that this should be seen as a general principle of linguistic meaning, not just an isolated exception.

While Wittgenstein pondered these matters in his rooms at Cambridge, linguists and anthropologists working with native Americans were coming to a similar conclusion. They found you couldn't properly translate native American languages into English: the categories didn't match up. The best-known example (the number of words the Eskimos have for 'snow') may be apocryphal, but the principle extends to more basic linguistic categories involving, for instance, the use of tenses or the distinction between the active and passive voices. The categories didn't match up because in fundamental ways native Americans didn't experience the world in the same way as English-speakers. And one of these linguists, Benjamin Lee Whorf, came up with a radical theory (now known as the 'Whorfian' or 'Sapir-Whorf' hypothesis) of how this came about: maybe, he suggested, language doesn't simply reflect the different ways in which different cultures see the world, but actually determines how they do so. Maybe, in short, language constructs rather than represents reality.

Such thinking can be readily transferred to aesthetics. It implies that, instead of reproducing an external, pre-existing reality, the role of art is to make available new ways of 'constituting our sense of reality', as another philosopher, Joanna Hodge, has put it. And, she continues, this 'makes it possible to claim that Dickens made fog an identifiable feature of experience, and that Van Gogh made sunflowers visible'. In other words, we experience the world in general, and sunflowers in particular, differently because of Van Gogh's paintings; it isn't that we always saw them like that, only nobody until Van Gogh managed to capture the way they looked. The real significance of painting, then, lies not in the artefact that is hung on the wall, but in the way of seeing the world that it instigates or constructs (for this reason Hodge calls this the 'constructivist' view of art). No longer are there absolute artistic standards rooted in external reality, in the way things are. Instead artistic value lies in the experience of the spectator, who is no longer detached from the artistic process but becomes an essential participant in it. In this way the basic assumptions of classical aesthetics are stood on their head.

You can see how this approach might apply to music. For one thing, it makes sense of the kind of hermeneutic criticism of music that I mentioned in Chapter 4, which consists of developing illuminating metaphors for particular compositions; such metaphors don't just represent something that you have already experienced, but lead you to experience the music differently. (In other words, they don't just reflect but change the way things are.) But the idea that music's meaning lies more in what it does than what it represents, if I can put it that way, has a broader application. The basic point is that it enables us to do justice to the aspect of music that has been most under-represented in writing (particularly academic writing) about it: its status as a *performance* art. And this in turn has ramifications for the way in which we study music, and especially the way in which we position ourselves in relation to it.

As a simple example of what is at issue, consider the classical orchestra. It consists of a team of specialists (violinists, oboists and so on), all working to a pre-existing blueprint or master plan (the score). Where there are several specialists in the same area, there are identifiable hierarchies and management lines (first and second violins, the leader). Throughout the eighteenth century one of the team members (normally a violinist or the harpsichordist) had overall control of the operation, but early in the nineteenth century this managerial role developed into a specialist career path (the conductor). Now held accountable for the success or failure of the entire operation, the manager acquired an executive status quite distinct from that of the other team members, with a remuneration package to match. In putting it this way, of course, I am drawing a parallel between the orchestra and other comparable socio-economic groups (change what is in the parentheses and we might be talking about a construction company, say). And if I were thinking of music as representation, I might say that the classical orchestra and its evolution reproduces the organizational structures of contemporary society.

To say that assumes, as classical aesthetics does, that music lies outside society. But what sense does it make to say that an orchestra lies outside society while a builder's firm is part of it? Isn't the orchestra, too, part of social structure? In which case, can't developments in orchestral practice contribute to, rather than merely reflect, broader social developments? Might not music indeed presage broader social developments? Hasn't the increased occurrence of conductorless orchestras and other *ad hoc* ensembles over the last two decades anticipated today's less hierarchical management styles and the development, in many fields, of alternatives to traditional institutional structures? I would not wish to be misunderstood; I am not suggesting that it is the role of music to provide a kind of early warning system for society (though such a suggestion has been made), any more than that it is its role to reflect society. The point is simply that, as I said, it is *part* of society, and as such as likely to be in the vanguard or to lag behind as any other part of society. And we are on much firmer ground when we try to understand the social transactions that are taking place within the practice of music—what is being *done*, in other words—than when we construct unverifiable hypotheses about what might be being represented.

An Inclusive Approach to Music

How might we apply this kind of thinking to a specific piece of music? A telling example, because of its political significance, is 'Nkosi Sikelel' iAfrica', the national anthem of the new South Africa. For years it was sung as an act of defiance against the apartheid regime and now, with the end of apartheid, it resonates with the hopes and aspirations, and fears, of the new South Africans and their sympathizers across the world.

In part this is a matter of straightforward association: 'Nkosi Sikelel' iAfrica' makes us think of South Africa. But only in part. For 'Nkosi Sikelel' iAfrica' also has a meaning that emerges from the act of performing it. Like all choral performance, from singing a hymn to chanting at a football match, it involves communal participation and interaction. Everybody has to listen to everyone else and move forward together. It doesn't just symbolize unity, it *enacts* it. And there is more. Through its block-like harmonic construction and regular phrasing, 'Nkosi Sikelel' iAfrica' creates a sense of stability and mutual dependence, with no one vocal part predominating over the others. (Compare the British national anthem, really just a tune plus accompaniment, or the

'Marseillaise', with its irregular, individualistic phrase construction.) Again, it lies audibly at the interface between
European traditions of 'common-practice' harmony and
African traditions of communal singing, which gives it an
inclusive quality entirely appropriate to the aspirations of the
new South Africa. In all these ways 'Nkosi Sikelel' iAfrica'
goes far beyond merely representing the new South Africa.
Enlisting music's ability to shape personal identity, 'Nkosi
Sikelel' iAfrica' actively contributes to the construction of
the community that is the new South Africa. In this sense,
singing it is a political act.

Few linguists today accept the 'strong' version of the Whorfian hypothesis, according to which language is the only thing
that determines conceptualization. Most, however, would accept that it is *one* of the things that determine conceptualization. And in the same way, it would be silly to claim that music
can *only* have meaning by virtue of what it does and not what
it represents. After all, 'Nkosi Sikelel' iAfrica' is not just a
political act; it is an imaginary object, too, a 'musical work'
with a history of its own. (It was composed in 1897 by Enoch
Sontonga, a teacher at a Methodist mission school in Johan-
nesburg.) When people sing 'Nkosi Sikelel' iAfrica' they are
not just constructing the new South Africa, then, they are also
reproducing what Sontonga wrote, just as when they play
the 'Hammerklavier' Sonata they are reproducing what
Beethoven wrote. There is a difference, though. For those
who sing or hear it, the meaning of 'Nkosi Sikelel' iAfrica' is
inextricably tied up with South Africa, but not in the same
way with Sontonga; knowing it was composed by Sontonga
may be interesting, but has little if anything to do with what it
means. But that isn't true of the 'Hammerklavier'. When we
listen to Beethoven's music we don't just listen to the sound
it makes. We hear it *as music by Beethoven*, hear it in relation
to the image of the composer that we build up through
listening to his music and reading about him. Indeed, if you

know it well, you are likely to hear a performance of the 'Hammerklavier' *as a performance of the 'Hammerklavier'*, re-lating what you hear to other performances of it that you have heard, or the critical commentary that has grown up around it.

It isn't, then, a question of either/or. It is a question of bal-ance. Music of the Western 'art' tradition, conceived within the guiding metaphor of the imaginary museum and ex-pressed in a notation of unparalleled comprehensiveness, is designed for reproduction. In other words, it is designed to be heard as a 'performance of' something that already exists and has its own identity and history, and to derive its meaning from being a 'performance of' it—from what is being repre-sented, that is to say, rather than what is being done. Seen this way, as Schoenberg once intemperately put it, 'the performer, for all his intolerable arrogance, is totally unnecessary except as his interpretations make the music understandable to an audience unfortunate enough not to be able to read it in print'. But this extreme statement of the aesthetics of representation is not really very tenable, for reasons that I have already repeatedly mentioned: the score conceals as much as it reveals, so that performers have a creative and not merely reproductive role in musical culture, and a glance at the musical market-place makes it obvious that many people's interest in music is largely an interest in its perform-ance. By itself, the aesthetics of representation is simply not an adequate basis for thinking about classical music. It leaves too much out.

And if this is the case of classical music, it is the more so of virtually all other musics. Far from being a reasonable stan-dard against which to judge other musics, the music of the Western 'art' tradition is a magnificently untypical special case—magnificent in its determination to defy time and create those most impossible of objects, musical works. If thinking of classical music as reproduction leaves too much out, in the case of most other musics—popular music, jazz, non-Western music—it leaves practically everything out. Such traditions are far more performance traditions than 'performance of' traditions, so to speak; jazz 'standards' like ''Round Midnight' have their own histories, like 'Nkosi Sikelel' iAfrica', but in the same way their meaning and value lies predominantly in what is enacted through performance. It could hardly be otherwise, when what is shared between performances of ''Round Midnight' is essentially a melodic and harmonic outline—a far cry from the score of, say, Beethoven's Ninth Symphony.

There is another point to be made, too. The artistic vision of classical aesthetics is in every way exclusive. It is based on the idea of the masterwork, whose value is intrinsic and eternal, regardless of whether anyone appreciates it or not (although in practice it is the musical institutions, as custodians of the imaginary museum, that decide what these eternal values are and which works embody them). Masterworks are created by the great composers (here the category of *Kleinmeister*, or not-so-great composer, comes into being) and they are reproduced in performance by specialist performers. (There is amateur performance, of course, particularly on the piano, but the 'Hammerklavier' Sonata effectively spelled the exclusion of the amateur from the masterwork tradition as 'great' music became harder and harder to play, with music for amateurs becoming an increasingly distinct, subordinate category.) And if you aren't a composer or a performer, or at any rate someone with a musical training, then you are a non-musician. You may go to concerts, buy records, even read books like this one, but that doesn't make you a musician. Classical aesthetics doesn't recognize you as a stakeholder. By contrast, an approach that is based on the activity of music—of composing it, performing it, listening to it, loving it, hating it, in short, *doing* it—brings everyone involved in music into the picture.

And this takes us back to the issue of music history which I raised at the end of the previous chapter. Traditionally, histories of music have been histories of musical compositions. What I want to draw attention to is not just the 'stepping-stone' approach; it's the whole emphasis on the production rather than the reception of music. You can see that this follows on from the 'picture' view of art, and indeed from the basic linguistic facts that I talked about in Chapter 1. The assumption is in effect that if you can explain composing, the first term of the National Curriculum trichotomy, then performing and appraising will look after themselves. But the 'constructivist' view of art turns this upside down, because it sees the primary role of art as to construct and communicate new modes of perception; that is where the historical process lies. Seen this way, the history of art is really a history of the changing ways in which people have seen things.

All this translates easily to music; we would say that Beethoven, Mahler, Steve Reich, Mike Oldfield, even Peter Gabriel didn't so much give us new things to hear as new ways of hearing things. Admittedly, in music it is a bit harder to define what we mean by 'reception', because we have both performers and listeners to deal with, rather than just spectators as in the case of painting. But performers and listeners (and for that matter writers on music, who are themselves sometimes performers and invariably, I suppose, listeners) are all involved in the same process: the interpretation of music. If the continuity of history lies in the story of how people have perceived things, then, we might reasonably expect interpretation—performance, listening, writing—to lie at the centre of music history, rather than on its margins. And a history that is based on reception would replace the orderly chronologies of the textbooks with an elaborate crisscrossing of influences and reminiscences as music leapfrogs from one era to another, from one corner of the globe to the opposite, or from 'high' art to 'low' art and back again. (Consider, as examples, the Paris-based phenomenon of 'world beat', in which traditional musics from Africa and elsewhere were given a 1980s pop music treatment and released to new international markets, the Spanish monks of Santo Domingo de Silos whose renditions of Gregorian chant brought EMI huge sales in 1994, or more recently the Medieval Babes with their pop-style promotion of medieval music; no wonder they were promptly dubbed the 'Old Spice Girls'.) These things do not happen by accident. They happen because the music of one time and place satisfies the needs, desires, or aspirations of another time and place. From the perspective of reception, it is musical needs, desires, and aspirations that form the stuff of history.

As in the case of the 'picture' and 'constructivist' views of art, what we need is balance; we need *both* composition-based and reception-based approaches to music, for the two work in a kind of counterpoint. (In other words what there is to hear determines what people want to hear, and what people want to hear determines what there is to hear.) And again, one of the reasons that we need a reception-based approach is because it is inclusive. Instead of the detached, non-participant viewpoint of the traditional histories and appreciation texts, the reception-based approach says that we can best understand music by being in the middle of it. It says that the starting-point must be how we (and that includes you and me) actually use, internalize, or otherwise care about music, whether by going to concerts or discos, relaxing to it in the sitting-room, or whistling it at work. It avoids prescriptive judgements, and in particular prescriptive judgements inherited from another age, about what we (and that means *you*) ought to listen to and how. It assumes that to study music is to study your own participation in it—to study yourself, as I put it at the end of the last chapter. And it will become clear, in the next chapter, that this insight has been a driving force in the dramatic changes that have taken place during recent years in academic thinking about music.

6 Music and the Academy

How We Got Into It . . .

In 1985 the musicologist Joseph Kerman—then a professor of music at Berkeley, and before that at Oxford—published a book called *Contemplating Music*. (Or at least that is what the American edition was called; the British edition appeared under the matter-of-fact title *Musicology*.) It was a highly personal, not to say personalized, account of the academic study of music—a history of musicology in terms of its most famous, or at least notorious, practitioners. Musicologists read it avidly for its gossip value. But it had a more serious purpose, too. It offered a kind of social history of musicology, relating the development of the discipline during his lifetime to the broader academic and institutional trends of the period.

And 'development' is the right word. In the medieval curriculum the study of music (conceived very much as a theoretical rather than a practical discipline) occupied pride of place, along with mathematics, grammar, and rhetoric. Thereafter the discipline suffered a long, sad decline. In the first half of the twentieth century music could be studied as a practical skill in conservatories, but only a handful of universities offered it. After the Second World War, however, there was a rapid expansion of the universities on both sides of the Atlantic, and it was in this context that the academic study of music became established as a subject in its own right (an academic study which, however, is almost invariably combined with practical performance, in a way that the medieval discipline was not). Kerman in effect argued that the agenda of musicology was the result of the institutional context within which it had developed. And instead of taking this for granted, he encouraged its practitioners to reflect on why they did what they did. In a word—Kerman's word—he advocated a 'critical' approach to the discipline, in place of what he saw as the prevailingly unreflective or 'positivist' approach. Kerman's book was widely read, and these two terms—one good, one bad—provide a framework for understanding a decade of change. As will become clear, however, the outcome was a musicology that was 'critical' in a sense distinctly different from what Kerman had in mind.

In order to explain what Kerman was attacking in the musicology of the day, I need to provide an overview of the discipline as a whole. And this immediately raises issues of academic geography. In what follows I shall concentrate on musicology in the English-speaking countries (there are major differences in practice and thinking in continental Europe, for example). But even then there is a complication. For the British and, on the whole, Australasians, 'musicology' is an inclusive term: music theorists and ethnomusicologists, to whom I shall return, are all musicologists, while music historians call themselves either that, or 'historical musicologists'. In North America, by contrast, music historians call themselves musicologists, thereby distinguishing themselves from music theorists and ethnomusicologists. The distinction also matters more than it does in Britain. American scholars clearly identify themselves as musicologists, music theorists, or ethnomusicologists; each group has a different professional association, and job advertisements normally specify which of the three is wanted. (In Britain people generally just advertise a lectureship in music.) To borrow a phrase from Bernard Shaw, it is a classic instance of Britain and America being divided by a common language.

Having said all this, historical musicologists (or musicologists as I shall from now on call them, for concision) are much the largest of the groups in numerical terms, and this gives them a certain dominance within the discipline as a whole. Not surprisingly, then, it was primarily at them that Kerman directed his attack. It had two main prongs, corresponding to the two main areas in which musicologists work, though in each case the message was the same. The first area is the one anticipated by Beethoven when he tried without success to interest publishers in producing a complete and authoritative edition of his own music. As I said, it would have been authoritative in two senses: rectifying the errors in, and contradictions between, the many different editions in which his works had appeared; and allowing him to define once and for all his final intentions with respect to each work. And although Beethoven's plan never came to fruition, it in effect provided a model for the most ambitious project of twentieth-century musicology: the production of authoritative editions of both individual composers' music and national repertories. This work continues today, but without quite the confidence that attended it in the past.

There are two problems with this project: first, that it is hard, and second, that it is impossible. The first problem arises out of the multiplicity of sources in which most music, particularly early music, exists, and the fact that these sources are generally flawed, incomplete, and contradictory. Suppose you are trying to edit an early fifteenth-century French *chanson* (song). The composer's original manuscript has disappeared. However, you know of five other manuscripts containing this *chanson*, dating from between thirty and fifty years later. Each is slightly different from the others, and all but one contain an improbable reading of a particular passage that looks like a copyist's error. And what looks like the best reading is actually the latest. How do you set about reconstructing what the composer wrote? On the basis that each manuscript was copied from another manuscript—which may or may not have survived—you try to construct a stemma, a kind of family tree showing which manuscript was copied from which other manuscript, in the hope that you will be able to work out which version or versions are closest to the composer's lost original. Some of the manuscripts in the stemma may be purely hypothetical (for instance, when the similarities between manuscript D and manuscript G suggest that they must have both been copied from another manuscript, now lost), and those that *do* exist will probably be scattered around different libraries in France, Britain, America, and perhaps Japan.

All this means that the editions of medieval music you see on the library shelf represent a massive amount of spadework, a good deal of scholarly judgement, and usually a generous helping of guesswork. And it is not just medieval music that requires such editing, though in general the older the music, the more drastic the editorial problems. Even those flagships of the repertory, the Beethoven symphonies, present difficulties. Astonishing as it may seem, it is only as I write, in the closing years of the millenium, that they are beginning to appear in editions which for the first time eliminate the quite blatant misreadings that crept into the early editions, for example when an engraver placed a note on the wrong line of the stave and so produced a striking discord that has been reverently reproduced by performers ever since. (Jonathan Del Mar's recent edition of the Ninth Symphony amply illustrates the embarrassing fact that some of the most imaginative and original moments in the canon have been the result of printers' errors.)

The second problem emerges when music survives, as nineteenth- and twentieth-century music not infrequently does, in a number of versions all of which carry the imprint of the composer's authority in one way or another. For a piano piece by Chopin, you may well have the composer's autograph (that is, a score in his own hand); copies made for sending to publishers; publisher's proofs, with autograph corrections; and the first printed edition, based on the proofs. In fact there may be three first editions from three different publishers (one each in France, England, and Germany, say). And the three published editions are not quite the same, because the copies sent to the publisher weren't quite the same (even though we have reason to think that Chopin checked all of them), or because Chopin made the proof corrections slightly differently in each case, or both. When this happens, which of the three versions is right? The last, because it represents the composer's most considered intentions? The first, because it is closest to his original conception? And what happens when, as is sometimes the case with Chopin, you then find a number of copies which he used when teaching his pupils, each of which contains different autograph annotations? Do we assume that Chopin was just making the music easier to play for an indifferent pupil, and accordingly discount the annotations? But maybe he thought he was improving the music? How would we know?

Situations like this are not hard to resolve, they are impossible. This is because the idea of resolving them is predicated on the assumption that Chopin was aiming throughout at a single authoritative version of the music which, once established, would stand for all time and render all other versions false. And there is no reason to believe that Chopin was aiming at any such thing. On the contrary, contemporary accounts make it clear that pianist-composers like Chopin and, in particular, Liszt tended to play their music slightly differently every time. (In Liszt's case, it wasn't only his own music that got this treatment; there was a joke that his finest performances were when he was sight-reading, because that was the only time that he ever played the music as written.) The Beethovenian model of the authoritative edition, rooted as it is in the kind of thinking I described in Chapter 2, simply doesn't fit Chopin and Liszt; there is no single, authoritative version of their music. And if this is the case of Chopin and Liszt, whose careers coincided with the institution of the musical museum, it is the more so of earlier composers.

Here is the source of the loss of confidence to which I referred. It's not just that producing authoritative editions is hard; or that they can never be more than provisional, since other scholars will reach different judgements or make different guesses; it's that, in the case of many and arguably all composers, there is something wrong with the basic conception of the task. But that doesn't mean that the work of collating multiple, scattered sources into modern, usable editions isn't worth while and indeed absolutely necessary. It just means that, like painting the Forth bridge, the job is never finished. And this wasn't the basis of Kerman's complaint. What he objected to was that when musicologists had finished editing one piece of music, they simply went on to the next. They didn't use their hard-won knowledge of the music as the basis for critical engagement with it—for the attempt, which Kerman saw as fundamental to musicology, to reach an understanding of the music of the past both for its own sake (that is to say, aesthetically) and for what it might contribute to an understanding of the social and historical context from which it came. They didn't, in other words, treat editing as something that contributed to musicology as a broad humanities discipline. They behaved rather like a pianist who practises scales but never plays pieces. It is this kind of mechanical application of technique that Kerman was highlighting when he used the pejorative term 'positivist'.

The other main area of musicological activity, corresponding to the second prong of Kerman's attack, might be described as contextual studies. Here the primary concern is not with the music as such, but with the social and historical circumstances that gave rise to it. This might range from the correct dating of the music and identification of the composer (perhaps to be verified through a combination of stylistic and archival evidence) to the purposes for which the music was written, its function in relation to contemporary economic or political structures, or the position of the composer and other musicians in society. In essence Kerman's complaint was the same as the one he levelled at the editors: there was nothing wrong with this kind of work as far as it went, but what was the point of it if it wasn't applied as a source of new insights about the music *as music*? Just like the editors, he said, archival scholars were building up knowledge, but to no apparent purpose. When were they going to get past the preliminaries and become critically engaged with the music? When were they going to stop evading the real issues of musicology as a humane discipline?

At first sight, it is curious that Kerman also directed the same complaint at music theory, the subdiscipline of musicology (or parallel discipline, if you prefer) whose specific aim is to engage with the music as music—that is to say, in its own right and on its own terms, as opposed to in terms of manuscript transmission, social context, or whatever. It is no accident that the idea of engaging with the music in its own right and on its own terms echoes the nineteenth-century thinking about music that I explained in Chapter 2. Music theory as we know it today, and in particular the practical application of theory that we call 'analysis', emerged from the ferment of ideas that surrounded the reception of Beethoven's music. I mentioned the way in which people tried to discover or invent some underlying plot or narrative which would explain the music's apparent contradictions and moments of incoherence, and I cited as an example Fröhlich's interpretation of the Ninth Symphony as a kind of self-portrait in music. This is an example of hermeneutic criticism, the construction of an illuminating metaphor that contributes to the experience of the music—a style of criticism very different from what we think of today as theory and analysis.

But the underlying plot or narrative in question might have a more abstract, structural nature. This applies, for instance, to the system of analysis developed by Heinrich Schenker. When he analysed the 'Ode to Joy' theme from the Ninth Symphony, Schenker did a kind of reverse engineering job: he reduced it to a series of basic melodic and harmonic patterns, showing how these basic patterns were elaborated in the music Beethoven actually wrote. (You can see part of his analysis in Fig. 17. At the top, marked 'Fgd.' for 'Foreground', is the first part of Beethoven's theme. Underneath it is the '2nd level', at which each phrase is reduced to three notes plus harmonic support. There is also a '1st level', which I have not shown, at which all of this is represented by a single note. The core of Schenkerian theory is the set of rules that specify how

Fig. 17. Schenker's analysis of the 'Ode to Joy' (*Der freie Satz*, ii, Fig. 109, e3)

you get from one level to another.) This kind of working model of the music wasn't intended to represent the chronology of Beethoven's composition of it. Rather it enabled you to understand the music in a way you otherwise couldn't. More specifically, it explained the moments of apparent incoherence as purely *superficial* phenomena resulting from the elaboration of the *underlying structure*; it allowed you to hear 'through' the *surface* to what lay underneath.

As the italics show, there is a metaphor at work here (you could say that Beethoven's music is being likened to a fabric that is thrown over a supporting frame, or maybe an animal's skin supported by its musculature and skeleton). But the metaphor is a highly regulated one, not something invented just for this piece; it was Schenker's theory, the truth of which he made it his life's work to demonstrate, that *all* music (or at least all great music, which for him meant Western 'art' music from Bach to Brahms) could and should be understood this way. Already, then, issues of value have entered into the equation. But in truth they were there from the start, for the whole point of trying to explain Beethoven's music in the first place was to show how it was really the product of genius despite appearances to the contrary. Schenkerian analysis—and the point applies to analysis in general—didn't, then, ask whether the music of Bach, Beethoven, and Brahms was of value. It *assumed* the music was of value, and tried to demonstrate this by showing how the music really was coherent, provided you dug down deep enough. It was, in short, an apologetic discipline, in the sense of being designed to defend a valued repertory, to underwrite its canonic status.

And this basic orientation has begun to be questioned only very recently, despite the many technical changes that theory and analysis have undergone over the years. In the decades after the Second World War, it was the hard sciences that occupied pride of place in the American academy; fringe disciplines, like music theory, tried to make themselves look as 'hard' as possible by adopting scientific language and symbol systems. Intuition and emotionally loaded language were ruthlessly eliminated. In their place came mathematical and computational approaches (there were even attempts around 1970 to implement Schenkerian analysis as a computer programme). And the result was that theory and analysis became increasingly technical, increasingly incomprehensible to anyone except specialists. It was Kerman's view, and that of a number of other commentators, that it had ended up substituting its own scientific jargon for the personal, living experience of music that had presumably drawn the theorists to it in the first place. (Kerman summarized his feelings in the title of a widely read article: 'How we got into analysis, and how to get out'.) In this way, then, theorists were just as guilty of refusing to engage critically with the music as musicologists. In fact their guilt was the greater: instead of just deferring such engagement, like the musicologists, the theorists proclaimed it unnecessary or even philosophically suspect.

You don't change the world by being even-handed and balanced. Kerman's view of musicology was a highly personal one; his characterization of theory and analysis was something of a caricature, and his account of Schenkerian analysis was a travesty. Nevertheless, people working in all areas of the discipline devoured Kerman's book greedily, not just to see what (if anything) Kerman had said about them personally, but because he articulated a widely shared perception that the interface between musicology and music, between the academic discipline and the human experience, was not everything it could be.

. . . *And How to Get Out*

How then might there be a better interface between music and the academy? One kind of answer is presented by the historical performance movement, which developed rapidly in the decade or two before Kerman's book appeared. The basic idea of historical performance (or historically informed performance, as it should really be called) is deceptively simple: you should play the music of the past in the way that it would originally have been played.

This made obvious sense at a time when it was thought perfectly normal to play Bach on the piano and baroque oboe sonatas on modern instruments, or to play Mozart symphonies using the same size of orchestra as for Brahms. After all, Bach wrote his keyboard music for harpsichord or clavichord, both of which had a completely different sound and touch from the piano (which had not yet been invented); baroque oboes, with just a few keys, are so different from the modern instrument that you virtually have to relearn your technique if you go from the one to the other. And Mozart's symphonies were originally played by far smaller groups than the twentieth-century symphony orchestra. What justification could there be for using the same modern, standardized instruments and ensembles for all music, regardless of its origins? How could you claim to understand Bach's or Mozart's music if you had never heard it played as the composer intended? And this applied not just to the instruments but equally to the way they were played, for instance in terms of dynamic shaping, articulation, and ornamentation. All these aspects of performance have changed significantly through the ages, and the only way they can be reconstructed is through in-depth study of period treatises. This is where musicologists have had an essential contribution to make to performance.

The historical performance movement developed by stages from a rather precious, open-toed sandal image in the first half of the twentieth century, via the erudite but pedestrian performances put out under the German 'Archiv' record label in the 1950s and 1960s, to a kind of musical counter-culture in the 1970s. To call it that makes it sound a bit like contemporary rock music, and the comparison is appropriate: 'historical' performers formed their own groups, generally playing medieval and early renaissance music, and hit the road in much the same way as rock bands. And it was when the charismatic but short-lived David Munrow topped the bill that historical performance started to attract real audiences. Before going to university, Munrow went to South America, and brought back armfuls of ethnic instruments with him. He proceeded to use these with abandon on stage— and with impunity, too, since there was often no way of telling what instruments the music had originally been played on. More to the point, perhaps, he brought to 'early music', as people now called it, a flexibility of approach and an extrovert presentation that, again, resembled contemporary rock more than the scholarly ambience of traditional historical performance.

Nowadays historical performance is accepted within the academy; you can study baroque oboe at many conservatories, and the fact that you can hear both 'historical' and 'unhistorical' performances of Bach or Mozart has become a fact of life in a pluralistic culture where different musical traditions run side by side. But the transformation was not achieved without a struggle, and the 'authenticity' debate which raged throughout the 1980s was the most lively, not to say vitriolic, in the recent history of either musicology or performance. As a slogan, 'authenticity' neatly combined two things. On the one hand, the claim was that performance on the appropriate period instruments, based on the performance practices codified in historical treatises, was 'authentic' in the sense of being historically correct. On the other, the term 'authenticity' brought into play all those positive connotations I talked about in the first chapter of this book—the idea of being sincere, genuine, true to yourself. In this way, if you played Bach on the piano—if your performance wasn't 'authentic'—then you weren't simply wrong in a scholarly sense: you were wrong in a moral sense too. You were tarred with the same brush as the Monkees.

In many ways the battle between the 'authentic' performers and the musical establishment is reminiscent of the Campaign for Real Ale (CAMRA) which took place in Britain at around the same time. CAMRA opposed the standardized products of the big brewers and aimed to revive old-fashioned, regional beer-making in all its delightful idiosyncracy; in essence the historical performance movement aimed at the same. And both were largely successful. 'Historical' performance is not only accepted in the academy, but has also steadily extended its reach towards the present day. At the time of writing, the front line lies in the first decades of the twentieth century, as exemplified by the 'authentic' performances of Elgar's symphonies by the New Queen's Hall Orchestra, a re-creation of the pre-war orchestra with which Elgar himself recorded them. Increasingly, then, 'historical performance' refers not so much to the music you play, but to the approach you bring to it.

And what is that approach? More often than not, the advocates of historical performance (which generally means the historical performers themselves, for many are highly articulate) have defined it as playing the music as the composer intended it. The problem with this formulation is of course that there is generally no way of finding out what the composer intended, other than what you can deduce from what he or she wrote. So an alternative formulation is: playing the music as it might have been played in a good performance of the period. The problem with *this* formulation is the one I discussed in Chapter 4, with reference to Alessandro Moreschi. Notation captures very little about performance style; that is not its job. When words are added to it, as in the period treatises, the result is usually a series of tantalizingly disconnected clues which you have to link together through the exercise of judgement, imagination, guesswork, and musical intuition. But all of these, of course, reflect your own training and experience as a musician at the turn of the twenty-first century. You cannot escape your own time. And in this way the whole authenticity project, as presented by its advocates, is rather like the authoritative editions project: not so much hard as impossible.

Richard Taruskin, another professor at Berkeley who combines extensive experience in historical performance with his wide-ranging academic activities, has put forward a persuasive critique of the authenticity project, whose starting-point is its apparent impossibility, the fact that you simply cannot know how music was performed before the twentieth century. He accepts the speculative nature of historical performers' interpretation of the documentary evidence. But what he emphasizes is the way in which historical performers have learnt to reflect on and interrogate their own practices in light of this evidence. They *think* about performance in a way that performers working in a continuous tradition do not have occasion to. And the fact that the evidence is always fragmentary and usually contradictory actually gives historical performers great freedom of interpretation. Taruskin even emphasizes the way in which so-called historical performance in fact embodies many of the qualities of twentieth-century composition—the streamlined textures and motor drive of Stravinsky's music, for example. Seen this way, he concludes, 'authentic' performance is authentic because it expresses twentieth-century musicianship, and not because of possibly spurious (and certainly undecidable) claims of historical correctness.

Further evidence that Taruskin is right comes from the way in which performers treat historical recordings. From about 1900 you can actually *hear* period performance, in many cases by the composer (Elgar conducting his symphonies, Debussy and Bartók playing their piano music, and so on). Modern performers listen to these recordings. But they do not imitate them, in the way that look-alike bands and Elvis impersonators imitate their models, although this would be the obvious thing to do if they *really* wanted to play the music as the composer intended it. Rather, they claim to extrapolate the stylistic principles embodied in the performances on the records, and then re-create the music on that basis. (This claim has, for instance, been advanced by John Boyden, the artistic director of the New Queen's Hall Orchestra.) But that is a convoluted argument. It is hard to avoid the conclusion that its primary purpose is to safeguard the interpretive freedom, the creativity, which performers and audiences both value, but which our perversely conflicted language for performance does not allow us openly to articulate; hence the cloak of scholarship in which historical performance is shrouded.

In demythologizing the scholarly rhetoric of (so-called) historical performance, Taruskin has placed performance style at the centre of music history; never again, perhaps, will it be possible to publish a 'history of twentieth-century music' that considers only twentieth-century composition, ignoring twentieth-century performance. And other recent initiatives in the study of performance are tending in the same direction: techniques borrowed from experimental psychology are enabling musicologists and theorists to study recorded performances in much the same sense that they have up to now studied scores, so helping to rectify the unbalanced approach that I have repeatedly complained about in this book. This is one way in which the poor fit between music and musicology diagnosed by Kerman is being addressed. But when he called for musicologists to transcend their positivism and engage critically with music—when he called, as he put it, for a 'musicology oriented towards criticism'—Kerman had something else in mind.

The truth is probably that the best examples of what he had in mind were his own books on a series of topics as diverse as sixteenth-century music, Beethoven's string quartets, and opera. Each of these books brought together a variety of contextual and analytical approaches, but what distinguished them was the way in which these approaches were brought to bear on the music itself. What I mean by this is that they aimed to give the reader a more informed, more sensitive appreciation of the music than he or she would otherwise have had. They aimed, like hermeneutic analysis (but with the full benefit of historical and analytical scholarship), to contribute to the experience of the music. In this way they were 'critical' in the same sense as traditional literary criticism (and one of Kerman's aims was clearly to give musicology some of the intellectual stature of such well-established humanities disciplines as the study of literature and history). And, as I said, in the decade following the publication of *Contemplating Music* musicologists responded to Kerman's call for a critical orientation. The manner in which they did so, however, perhaps owed less to Kerman's own prescription than to developments in the third and last of the major musicological subdisciplines, namely ethnomusicology.

Musicologists and music theorists see ethnomusicology as the study of the music they don't study; ethnomusicologists see it as the study of *all* music in terms of its social and cultural context, embracing production, reception, and signification. (Not surprisingly, then, the study of popular music entered ethnomusicology well before it reached either musicology or music theory.) Because of its close links with other human sciences, particularly anthropology, ethnomusicology tends to be more responsive than musicology or music theory to trends outside the discipline, and in the postwar years it was affected not only by the 'hard science' orientation I previously referred to, but also by the various structuralist approaches that came out of Europe in the 1970s. In the 1980s, however, it began to develop a new orientation. Central to this was the realization that, if you were a Western ethnomusicologist coming to a non-Western society, you could not occupy the position of a detached observer. Your own status as a Westerner gave you a particular orientation towards the society you were observing, and conversely members of that society responded to your presence in ways that changed what they did. Just by being there you perturbed the phenomena you were observing, and you had to factor that into your interpretation of what you saw and heard.

And there was another point. Ethnomusicologists often found themselves working with societies engaged in transforming their own cultural identity, perhaps in pursuit of Westernization and industrialization. Under such circumstances, the scholarly objectives of recording and maintaining a traditional culture might place ethnomusicologists on a collision course with their informants—or alternatively they might find themselves siding with their informants against the government on whose cooperation their continued research depended. Worse, ethnomusicologists might discover clear evidence that controverted cherished and even politically important beliefs. A prime example is Kay Kaufman Shelemay's work with the Beta Israel community of Ethiopia. The Beta Israel believed themselves to be of Jewish origin, and on the basis of this had been able to secure emigration to Israel, thereby escaping the ravages of the Ethiopian civil war. But Shelemay's study of the Beta Israel liturgy clearly demonstrated that its origins were Christian, not Jewish; the Beta Israel are not really of Jewish origin at all. Should Shelemay publish her results? To do so might damage the relationship that the Beta Israel had forged with the State of Israel; to do otherwise would be to jeopardize her own integrity as a scholar.

Situations like this led ethnomusicologists to reflect on and evaluate their own position in a way that musicologists and music theorists, and even historical performers, did not. It led them not just to be critical, but to be *self*-critical. They were engaged with the music that they studied not just in an aesthetic sense (the kind of critical appreciation that Kerman had in mind), but politically; in the terminology I used in the previous chapter, musicology gave them the power not just to represent things but to *do* them, and they had to take responsibility for what they did. Like singing 'Nkosi Sikelel' iAfrica', musicology was a political act. And when the response to Kerman's call to criticism came, it was this kind of critical orientation, rather than the one Kerman had in mind, that characterized it.

7 Music and Gender

The Invisible Sex

During the Thatcher/Reagan years, it was received wisdom that ideology was what the other guy had. Capitalist democracy wasn't an ideology, it was just the way things were; it was the Russians who had ideology, and look what happened to *them*. (There is a comparison with the idea that Blacks but not Whites 'have' race, women but not men 'have' gender, and so on.) But an ideology is a system of beliefs which is transparent, which represents itself as just 'the way things are', and seen this way it is the apparent naturalness of capitalist democracy that demonstrates its ideological status. And since the 1930s there has been a rebellious subdiscipline of sociology called 'critical theory' whose avowed purpose is to expose the workings of ideology in everyday life, revealing 'uncritically' accepted beliefs and so returning to individuals the power to decide for themselves what they will believe— for, by presenting themselves as simply 'the way things are', ideologies suppress the very existence of alternatives.

Critical theory had its origins in Marxism, but developed to become a comprehensive mode of culture critique whose effects have been felt in disciplines as varied as literary studies, film and media studies, art history—and, more recently, musicology. Theodor Adorno, one of the founders of critical theory, was not only a sociologist but also an accomplished musician (he studied composition with Schoenberg's most famous pupil, Alban Berg), and he wrote as much on music as he did on sociology. He is not an easy writer to read (and there are almost as many interpretations of his work as there are readers of it), but his books have been appearing steadily in translation over the last two decades and have contributed significantly to the emergence of the 'critical' viewpoint for which Kerman called. They have also contributed to the fact that this critical viewpoint, when it arrived, had a political, interventionist quality quite different from what Kerman had envisaged (and they form part of the background to the developments in ethnomusicology which I described in the last chapter).

Critical theory is in essence a theory of power, and it sees power largely in terms of the institutions through which it is channelled. Institutions, in other words, are crucial in naturalizing power structures, in making it seem as if the unequal distributions of power we see across the world must be just 'the way things are'. In musicology, this approach has stimulated historical research into the formation of the canon (the repertory of masterworks on display in the musical museum) and the role of musical institutions in constructing, maintaining, and naturalizing this canon. But you can see the process at work today in the most important of such institutions: those at which music is taught (schools, conservatories, and universities). It is most obvious in the repositioning of rock within the academy that is going on as I write. In the opening chapter I mentioned how the development of the CD led record companies to reissue their back lists of rock music. But of course not everything could be re-released, and so a process of selection went on which was in effect the first stage in deciding what rock music entered the canon. And the process was repeated within universities as ways were found of bringing rock within teaching practices designed for the classical tradition. The emerging canonic status within the curriculum of the Beatles, for instance, partly reflects the fact that you can talk about 'Because' or 'Here Comes the Sun' using the same kind of vocabulary you use of Schubert's songs, in a way that you can't with the Rolling Stones. (One reason for this is that what is characteristic about the Beatles's songs is largely composed into them—into the melodies and harmonies, and the way they link with the text—whereas what really made the Stones's songs different was the way they performed them. That is why it is the Beatles's music, not the Stones's, that you hear in 'easy listening' instrumental versions in elevators and airport departure lounges.)

An even more basic example of how educational institutions construct and naturalize musical culture is provided by what is sometimes revealingly termed 'ear training', a kind of conditioning that takes place at an early stage of conservatory or university education: students are taught to recognize such things as the notes of the scale, the chordal types of 'common-practice' harmony, and the basic formal schemes of the classical tradition (binary, ternary, sonata, and so on). When I say 'things', I mean the word literally: students are being inducted into the world of Western musicianship, in which music is made up of 'things' to hear, constructed out of notes in the same sense that houses are constructed out of bricks. And this has two results. The first is that music is transformed from being primarily something you *do* (but do not necessarily know how you do) to something you *know* (but may not necessarily do); in other words, it is embraced within the structures of the knowledge industry, and of a society which tends to value theory above practice. The second is that it becomes increasingly difficult to conceive that music might work in other ways, or to hear it properly if it does; the harder you listen, the more you hear it in terms of the notes and chords and

formal types of the Western tradition, and the less you can understand music that works primarily in terms of timbre and
texture, say. (This is what I call the 'Hong Kong taxi problem':
Cantonese is a tonal language, so that for instance 'gau' can
mean 'nine' or 'dog' depending on how high or low you say it,
and when the Cantonese don't at first understand what you
are saying they listen harder to the tones. But Westerners
have great difficulty in getting the tones right. The net result is
that if the taxi-driver doesn't catch where you want to go the
first time, he never will, and you should get out and look for
another taxi.)

At all levels, then, what you know about music can open
your ears to it or close them, make certain types of music
seem 'natural' and others not just inconceivable but, in effect,
inaudible. No wonder, then, that music education has become a political battleground on both sides of the Atlantic. I
have already mentioned the National Curriculum and GCSE,
the aim of which is to involve students in the creation and
understanding of music, rather than initiating them into a remote and élite masterwork tradition; Bach and Beethoven remain on the syllabus, to be sure, but they share it with the
Beatles (maybe not the Stones) and Balinese music. And in
1989 a working party of the College Music Society, the American university music teachers' association, made very similar recommendations for the undergraduate curriculum: it
needed to recognize the ethnic diversity of American society,
they said, and celebrate the resulting wealth of 'art' and popular traditions. In both Britain and America there was a back-
lash from those who identified the Western 'art' tradition with
civilization (or rather Civilization, as I put it in Chapter 3) and
saw the admission to the curriculum of multicultural arts as
a decline in educational standards. They talked about Bach
and Bowie, but what was really at issue was the role of an élite
culture in supporting the social and political status quo.

The 'critical' orientation that developed in musicology as

an oblique response to Kerman, then, had something of the political edge of critical theory, and it was only natural that a key area in this development should be gender studies. The history of music, as it is generally told, is conspicuous by the absence of women. The reason has more to do with the way history is told than with a lack of musical activity on women's part. Practically every Jane Austen heroine plays the piano; it was a standard social accomplishment in upper middle-class circles of the day. (If her lover or husband was musical, he probably played a melody instrument such as the flute or violin—with the consequence that when they played sonatas together she accompanied him, taking her lead from him, just as she was expected to do in other walks of life.) The point, then, is not that women did not play music, but that they played it at home. With few exceptions (the main one being the opera house) they were amateurs, performing for friends but not for money. And they rarely composed. Even Fanny Hensel, the prodigiously talented elder sister of Felix Mendelssohn, published only a few songs (they appeared under her brother's name), and surviving letters between them show the pressure she was under to conform to the social expectations of the day—which did not include composition.

All this resulted in a kind of vicious circle. Because women generally didn't compose, the essentializing assumption was made that, as women, they were constitutionally or even biologically incapable of it. As a result, the few women who *did* compose tended to adopt male pseudonyms, because they could get performances that way which they could not under their real names—but that, of course, only reinforced the vicious circle. And the even fewer women who composed openly found themselves in a no-win situation: the (male) reviewers of music by the French composer Cécile Chaminade, whose long life spanned the nineteenth and twentieth centuries, alternately complained that her music did not have the 'virility' of men's music, and that its virility was unbecoming in a woman. In this way women were active in music in those areas (performance, and in particular amateur performance) that the history books ignore, and they were largely frustrated in their attempts to work in those areas (primarily composition) that *are* recognized by the history books.

Things have changed, of course. Women became progressively more active as professional performers in the second half of the nineteenth and first half of the twentieth centuries. And in the twentieth century a significant number of female composers achieved internationally recognized stature, even if none of them have quite become household names: Amy Beach, Ruth Crawford Seeger, Elisabeth Lutyens, and Nicola Lefanu, for instance. But the problem has not gone away. On the contrary, sexism is rife in the music business. Despite the spectacular success of women in popular music, the popular music press is still inclined to assume that female stars do not conceive or create their own music; the 'disco-bimbo' image attached for a long time to Madonna, for instance, despite the well-documented fact that she actively co-authored the majority of her songs (though not, as it happens, 'Material Girl'). But the most spectacular example is that of the Vienna Philharmonic Orchestra, which in 1997, and in the face of mounting public protest, *confirmed* its policy of excluding all women—except harpists (the male harpist is virtually an endangered species). It thereby remained true to the dictum of its most famous conductor, Herbert von Karajan, that A women's place is in the kitchen, not in the symphony orchestra'.

One way for a 'critical' musicology to respond to this situation, obviously, is to champion the cause of women in music, not only through furthering the composition and performance of women's music (there are nowadays gazetteers of female composers, women's publishing cooperatives and record labels, and so forth) but also through developing new ways of writing history that more adequately recognize the activities of women. Both of these are ongoing projects, and face a fundamental problem that applies to women's studies in general: do you attempt to position women's music within the mainstream, thereby risking its being swamped by a predominantly male tradition, or do you promote it as a separate tradition of its own, as *women's* music, thereby risking marginalization within a male-dominated culture? (The generally accepted answer is that you do both.) But there is also another approach, which is to bring insights derived from feminism and gender studies to bear upon the canon of masterworks (and note the word, *master*works). From a musicological point of view it is this that has been of most significance, because it has become the model for a new kind of critical engagement with music.

Outing Music

That music and sex have something in common (that they are 'psychically next door', as musicologist Suzanne Cusick puts it) has never been much in doubt; consider the way we call music 'ravishing', so treating it as a kind of sexual partner— and an active one at that. (You don't ravish music; it ravishes you.) From this it is a short step to ask what gendered characteristics music might have—how composers have consciously or unconsciously constructed it as gendered, that is to say. This is in particular an obvious thing to do in the case of music concerned with the construction of bourgeois subjectivity, as I called it in Chapter 2. I have already explained how Beethoven's listeners and commentators often heard his music in terms of the depiction of an exceptional individual, generally identified within the composer himself; given that, it is not unreasonable to ask what role sexual characteristics might play in this depiction. And according to Susan McClary (who was not the first person to work in this area, but has been by far the most influential), Beethoven's music virtually shouts out the answer to this question.

The basic idea is very simple. Everybody comments on the assertive and heroic qualities of Beethoven's music. Sometimes, especially in his symphonic climaxes, there is something a bit obsessive (Pieter van den Toorn has called it 'crazy') about his interminable, repeated downbeats, like a succession of hammer blows: the music goes bang, bang, bang, and occasionally you have to ask yourself *why* Beethoven insists on banging away like this. In effect, McClary hears the music going bonk, bonk, bonk, and she asks herself why Beethoven insists on . . . well, you get the point. To be sure, the terminology is a bit different; McClary talks about pounding, about pelvic thrusts, even about rape. She famously described the final section of the first movement of Beethoven's Ninth as an 'unparalleled fusion of murderous rage and yet a kind of pleasure in its fulfillment . . . [F]inally [at the end of the symphony] Beethoven simply forces closure by bludgeoning . . . the piece to death.' You couldn't expect to compare Beethoven's Ninth Symphony to a sexual killer's fantasy with impunity in the world of 1980s musicology, though; McClary's approach stirred up almost as big a controversy as the 'authenticity' movement. The main objections might be summarized as 'Why sex?' and 'Hands off!', although they tended to be expressed at greater length and more vitriolically.

I shall come back in due course to the second objection. As regards the first, both the gendered terminology and the undercurrent of violence have a long history in descriptions of musical form, in particular that of the sonata—traditionally the genre of choice for serious, abstract music. For instance, the French composer Vincent d'Indy wrote in 1909 that a sonata's first idea (or theme) should embody such 'essential *masculine* characteristics' as 'force and energy, concision and clarity'. And he continued:

The *second* idea, in contrast, entirely gentle and of *melodic* grace, is affective almost always by means of its verbosity and modulatory vagueness of the eminently alluring *feminine*: supple and elegant, it spreads out progressively the curve of its ornamented melody.

On the one hand, masculine force and energy, concision and clarity; on the other, feminine grace and elegance, verbosity and vagueness (with an alluring hint of curvaceousness, too). You could hardly ask for a clearer example of gender stereotyping. Bear in mind, also, that whereas in a traditional sonata movement each theme initially appears in a different key, in the final section both themes come back in the key of the first; the first theme imposes its key on the second. Or as d'Indy put it, after the 'active battle of the development [the middle section of sonata form], the being of gentleness and weakness has to submit, whether by violence or by persuasion, to the conquest of the being of force and power'.

D'Indy, then, would evidently have known what McClary was talking about; expressed in his terms, her point is that in the Ninth Symphony Beethoven seems keener on violence than on persuasion. And in saying this McClary is expressing more pointedly what others have also felt. Cusick, for instance, complains of the way that Beethoven's insistent rhythms 'don't give me the choice I cherish'—whether in music or, she implies, in sex. (Beethoven, as she puts it, insists on always being on top.) And perhaps surprisingly, Cusick's liberated, late-twentieth-century words echo those of a staunch Victorian, Sir George Grove, who wrote in the first (1882) edition of his *Dictionary of Music and Musicians* of 'the strong, fierce, merciless coercion, with which Beethoven forces you along, and bows and bends you to his will'. The only real difference seems to be that, unlike Cusick, Grove enjoyed being forced, bowed, and bent; at least, I can detect no hint of resistance in his use of these terms.

Grove says this in the course of a comparison between Beethoven and Schubert which itself bears very much on issues of gender: 'compared with Beethoven', he writes,

'Schubert is as a woman to a man. For it must be confessed that one's attitude towards him is almost always that of sympathy, attraction, of love.' Now Grove had never met Schubert, who died in 1828, the year after Beethoven; it is the music, not the man, to which he is attributing these feminine qualities. And again McClary works out in detail something that Grove merely hints at. Or at least, she finds very different characteristics in Schubert's music (specifically, the second movement of his 'Unfinished' Symphony) from those she found in Beethoven's Ninth. To be sure, there are occasional heroic posturings, but Schubert undermines them, renders them unconvincing. The opening of the symphony, she says, 'invites us to forgo the security of a centered, stable tonality and, instead, to experience—and even *enjoy*—a flexible sense of self'. Whereas in Beethoven's symphonies the self

strives to define identity through the consolidation of ego boundaries . . . Schubert tends to disdain goal-oriented desire per se for the sake of a sustained image of pleasure and an open, flexible sense of self—both of which are quite alien to the constructions of masculinity then being adopted as natural, and also to musical form as commonly construed at the time.

Then she adds: 'In this, Schubert's movement resembles uncannily some of the narrative structures that gay writers and critics are exploring today.' And there we have it: Grove spoke of Schubert as a woman, but he meant something else, something that his Victorian sensibility would not permit him to speak out loud.

It wasn't so much McClary's interpretation of Schubert's music as constructing an alternative model of male subjectivity that made the shit hit the fan. It was rather a scholarly paper presented at the 1988 Annual Meeting of the American Musicological Society, in which Beethoven's most famous modern biographer, Maynard Solomon, cited a wealth of circumstantial detail showing that homosexuality featured prominently in the Viennese circles that Schubert frequented. And Solomon suggested that the composer was himself gay. Solomon's arguments were promptly rebutted and a virulent controversy ensued in the pages of the mainstream press as well as the specialist journals. The arguments and counter-arguments were inconclusive, as indeed they were bound to be, for nobody living in as repressive a society as early nineteenth-century Vienna could have been so foolish as to leave unambiguous evidence of what would certainly have been seen as sexual deviance. What was much more indicative was the manner in which the controversy was pursued, both by those who were eager to accept Solomon's arguments and those who were prepared to go to almost any lengths to refute them.

But indicative of what? The advertisement in Fig. 18 (in which Schubert's name duly appears) provides part of the answer. The title, 'Out Classics', refers to the practice which first became widespread in the late 1980s of 'outing' closet homosexuals (that is, exposing as homosexuals those public figures who kept their sexuality a secret and sometimes adopted a public stance of opposing homosexuality). If Solomon was right, then it was possible for the first time to claim one of the unassailably central figures of the canon for gay culture (the other composers featured on 'Out Classics' are at best on the margins of the canon—apart from Tchaikovsky, perhaps, and Chopin, whose inclusion is possibly based on a mistaken assumption that the novelist George Sand, with whom he lived, was a man). And what about the other side? Their point wasn't exactly that Schubert must have been heterosexual (or celibate, for that matter). It was that his music, like all music, had nothing to do with sexuality of any variety; it transcended it, and so inhabited an autonomous world of its own. This kind of 'Hands off!' approach reflects the kind of thinking I talked about in Chapter 2; it is tied up with the Beethoven myth. But now, from the point of view of gender politics, we

Fig. 18. Advertisement for 'Out Classics' (*Independent on Sunday*)

might see that myth a bit differently. For if the music that dominates the canon expresses a characteristically male, heterosexual construction of subjectivity—if McClary is right—then the myth of 'pure' music passes off male, heterosexual values as universal, while pretending that gender doesn't come into it. It is a classic case of ideology in action.

And here, going beyond specific issues of gender, we come

to the heart of the 'New' musicology, as the proponents of the post-Kerman 'critical' approach self-consciously called it—a name which inevitably has a rather short shelf-life. (In fact I would claim that it has passed its 'best before' date, and that the 'New' musicology is now part of the mainstream.) The name was coined by Lawrence Kramer in 1990, and he has perhaps spelt out its agenda more articulately than anyone else. Central to it is the rejection of music's claim to be autonomous of the world around it, and in particular to provide direct, unmediated access to absolute values of truth and beauty. This is on two grounds: first, that there are no such things as absolute values (all values are socially constructed), and second that there can be no such thing as unmediated access; our concepts, beliefs, and prior experiences are implicated in all our perceptions. The claim that there are absolute values which can be directly known is therefore an ideological one, with music being enlisted to its service. A musicology that is 'critical' in the sense of critical theory, that aims above all to expose ideology, must then demonstrate that music is replete with social and political meaning—that it is irreducibly 'worldly', to use one of Kramer's favourite terms.

Seen from this point of view, though, there looks to be a problem with McClary's own approach to music. For McClary writes in very much the same way as critics have always written about music: she says how it is. She writes from a traditionally constructed position of authority, as if she herself had some special access to the music's meaning. But as Kramer constantly reiterates, a genuinely critical, which is to say self-critical, musicology must avoid entrenched positions of authority; it must recognize its provisional nature, its own social constructedness. (In another of Kramer's favourite phrases, it must retain interpretive mobility.) It is ironic, then, that Kramer found himself attacked on very much the same grounds by an even 'Newer' musicologist, Gary Tomlinson, and the resulting exchange of views revealed much about the basic assumptions of each party. Tomlinson in effect accused

Kramer of being just another old-fashioned critic with an up-
dated vocabulary; when he comes to talk about the music,
Tomlinson complained, 'The inviolate security of his knowledge speaks the language of an older musicology'. In this way
Kramer ends up domesticating music, imposing his own
meanings on it (but imputing them to the music). He ends up
making music too easy to understand.

The vision that Tomlinson puts forward is arguably the
bleakest in musicology today. In any of its varieties, he says,
and whatever the appearances to the contrary, 'criticism'
means trying to understand music through detaching it from
its historical context. And it never *can* be detached from that
context without doing violence to it. The more we engage in
'close reading'—the attempt to engage with music *as music*—
the more we impose our own values on it, in a kind of aesthetic colonialism that assumes our ways of understanding to
be the only ways of understanding. Indeed, Tomlinson concludes, even to talk about 'music' is to create a spurious intimacy between ourselves and the historical or geographical
other. There is an austere logic to Tomlinson's arguments, but
they seem to lead to a dead end; they throw the baby out with
the bathwater, for (as Kramer retorts) 'the death of criticism
would follow on the death of what we currently think of as
music'. And Kramer adds pointedly: 'For some of us that
might seem too high a price to pay.'

But Tomlinson's vision of 'a musicology without music' (the
phrase is Kramer's, of course) has a pedigree. There is a strong
strain of cultural pessimism in critical theory, resulting from
the sense that ideology never *can* be fully rooted out, and in
the case of Tomlinson and other 'New' musicological pessimists it is perhaps reinforced by the widespread perception
I referred to earlier that classical music, in America at least, is
fading away. It seems to me, though, that part of Tomlinson's
problem is that he emphasizes the 'worldly' nature of music—
its entrapment, so to speak, within sociopolitical structures—

at the expense of its role as an agency of personal and social transformation. As I said at the beginning of this book, music is one of the means by which we *make* ourselves who we are, and the fact that the choice is never wholly our own is no reason for not valuing such freedom as we do have. In the remainder of this chapter, and in the Conclusion, I shall try to spell out this cautiously optimistic position in more detail, and I shall begin by returning to issues of music and gender.

Something We Do

I have already spoken about the way in which ethnomusicologists were led to theorize their own positions. Gender-oriented (feminist, gay, lesbian) musicology requires exactly the same thing: it means writing from a specifically gendered position. In particular, gay and lesbian musicology means writing from an explicitly gay or lesbian stance. It involves a kind of professional coming out. And this would have been professional suicide until around 1990, when conference papers and articles started appearing with titles like 'On a Lesbian Relationship with Music: A Serious Effort Not to Think Straight' (Suzanne Cusick) or 'Queer Thoughts on Country Music and k. d. lang' (Martha Mockus). Coming out is indeed the topic of Mockus's article: in 1992, after several years of ambivalence, the American country/rock singer k. d. lang publicly anounced that she was a lesbian, arguably the first mainstream performer to do so (Fig. 19). Musicology's coming out of the closet, then, was part of a broader cultural process.

A statement of coming out, whether made by a singer or a musicologist, is a performative act: like a promise, it isn't a report on something done elsewhere, it is the *doing* of it. That is what, in her article, Cusick says about music itself: we constantly tend to forget, she writes, that 'music (like sex . . .) is first of all something we *do*, we human beings, as a way of

Fig. 19. k. d. lang in performance

explaining, replicating, and reinforcing our relationship to the world, or our imagined notions of what possible relationships might exist'. And what Cusick says of music is equally true of her own musicology: the article, written in a highly personal manner quite distinct from that of her 'straight' publications on seventeenth-century Italian music, precisely tries to explain, replicate, and reinforce her experience of music and sexuality as being perhaps not just 'psychically next door' to one another but ultimately inseparable. Or it might be even more accurate to say that it *constructs* her experience of music and sexuality, in the same sense that McClary reads

Beethoven's and Schubert's music as constructing different models of male subjectivity.

There is a difference, though. Cusick's article is based on precisely the kind of critical self-evaluation that I described in the previous chapter. By contrast, McClary gives the impression of not theorizing her own position. That is what I meant when, echoing Kramer, I spoke of her writing from a traditionally constructed position of authority. Cusick's article doesn't lead you to ask 'But is music *really* inseparable from sex?' because her article doesn't reference an external reality in which this might or might not be the case; rather, it creates a vision, a way of experiencing the world, in which music simply *is* inseparable from sex. (You might find the vision unconvincing, or for that matter objectionable, but to complain that 'it's not really true' would be hardly more appropriate than in the case of a novel, say.) By contrast, McClary can be read as saying how the music really *is*, as if the meaning was really 'in' the music after all, just waiting to be discovered. And she has certainly been read as saying how Beethoven and Schubert really were; 'McClary's linkages between composers' hypothesized sensibilities and features in musical repertories remain grounded in essentialist thinking,' James Webster grumbles. He goes on to point out that Beethoven's music sometimes explores just those features that, in the case of Schubert, McClary associates with homosexuality. If there is something gay about third-related harmonies and idiosyncratic formal structures, he in effect asks (and many of McClary's critics have asked the same), how come we find them in the music of so unequivocally straight a composer as Beethoven?

But that last question only makes sense on the essentialist assumption that Webster is objecting to—that gay composers write gay music, and straight ones write straight music, because that's simply the way they are. (Figs. 20–1 illustrate how images of the two composers tend to conform to the same stereotypes.) By contrast, McClary is careful to explain that

Fig. 20. Joseph Teltscher, *Franz Schubert*, 1826, lithograph

the constructions of gendered subjectivity she is talking about are in principle available to any composer. In which case, if there are gay qualities in some of Beethoven's music, might that not be because, through music, he was exploring the gay side of his own psychological make-up? Mightn't that be one of the things we use and value music for? (Could that be what Grove was doing, knowingly or not?) And seen in this light, mightn't music be one of the ways in which we can learn to go beyond such black-and-white, essentializing categorizations

Fig. 21. Kaspar Clemens Zumbusch, *Beethoven Figure for the Vienna Beethoven Monument*, 1878, bronze, Vienna

as 'gay' or 'straight' and instead come to appreciate the complexities, the provisionalities, the light and shade of genuine human sexuality? In fact, aren't McClary's readings of the music of Beethoven and Schubert (and Monteverdi, and Laurie Anderson, and Madonna) illustrations of precisely the kind of performative engagement that Cusick describes in her article? To say this is to imply that the value of what McClary says lies not in its 'truth', in the sense of correlation with an external reality (Beethoven's music was *really* straight, Schubert's was *really* gay), but in its persuasiveness—and that in turn reflects our willingness to be persuaded, how much it matters to us that music might function as an arena for gender politics. The strength of feeling elicited by writing on music and gender, both for and against, suggests that just now, at the turn of the twenty-first century, it matters to us a good deal.

Of course there has to be something more to scholarship than just whether or not we want to believe its results. And one of the problems with McClary's readings, as I see it, is that they employ the vocabulary of sexuality to describe qualities of music that are polyvalent—that can be understood in a variety of ways, of which sexuality is just one. Ludwig Tieck, one of the originators of the Beethoven myth, described instrumental music as 'insatiate desire forever hieing forth and turning back on itself'; the metaphor is appropriate (think of the way in which classical music sets up goals, then tantalizes you by constantly postponing their fulfilment), but of course the desire doesn't necessarily have to be conceived as sexual. Again, the way that Beethoven sometimes assaults, batters, and finally obliterates his musical materials makes it easy to believe that his music has something—something not very nice—to say about early nineteenth-century concepts of authority and subordination. But McClary's coital metaphors aren't the only way this could have been expressed.

More generally, we might say that what is at issue in the music of Beethoven and Schubert is the very idea of difference, of standard versus other. In any culture male versus female is likely to be a primary expression of this, but in Ira Gershwin's words, 'it ain't necessarily so'; race and religion, for instance, are equally good candidates. (To be fair to McClary, she has herself speculated along such lines, but inevitably it is the talk of pounding, pelvic thrusts, and rape that everyone remembers.) In its patterns of similarity and difference, divergence and convergence, conflict and resolution, music has a generality that is inevitably distorted by the elaboration of any individual metaphor we use for it. Metaphors focus music. They give a specific expression to its latent qualities. But these latent qualities must in the first place be there in the music, in its patterns of similarity, divergence, and so on; otherwise the metaphor will be entirely unpersuasive. (Try imagining the final section of the first movement of Beethoven's Ninth as the depiction of a plane journey across the Australian bush, and you will see what I mean.) So even if McClary's interpretations are are subjective, they cannot be *just* subjective. And the way in which metaphor gives specific expression to music contains the answer to the paradox I mentioned at the end of Chapter 2, that (in Scott Burnham's words) 'music no longer in need of words now seems more than ever in need of words'. Music is pregnant with meaning; it does not just reflect verbal meaning. But words function, so to speak, as music's midwife. Words transform latent meaning into actual meaning; they form the link between work and world. To borrow Kramer's term, they are the agent of music's worldliness.

In this way, interpretations of music like McClary's (and Cusick's, and many others) open up its ability to function as an arena for the negotiation of gender politics, and indeed of other personal and interpersonal values. Philip Brett calls music 'an enclave in our society—a sisterhood or brotherhood of lovers, music lovers, united by an unmediated form of communication that is only by imperfect analogy called a language, "the" language of feeling'. And certainly music has a record of offering a privileged zone for the construction of gender identities barely sustainable in the world outside; think of Little Richard or Michael Jackson. But this history goes back much further, and I am not just referring to the castrati. In late eighteenth- and early nineteenth-century Europe, music was thought of as an intrinsically feminine activity, and this applied especially to such intimate and domestic genres as the song with piano accompaniment. Men who intruded on such territory did so at some risk to their sexual identity, and the exaggeratedly 'masculine' nature of music in the Beethovenian tradition has sometimes been interpreted in terms of an overcompensation for this—a kind of repressed homosexual panic. The genre of art song in the first half of the nineteenth century, then, constituted an arena strongly marked by sexual politics: on the one hand it provided a rare opportunity for men to explore a side of their nature otherwise strictly off limits, but on the other it threatened their identity. It was a kind of no man's land.

Now imagine in this arena the effect of the song cycle *Frauenliebe und -leben* (A woman's love and life), composed by Robert Schumann to texts by Adelbert von Chamisso. The words construct a kind of fictive autobiography, the story of a woman who falls in love with her ideal man, marries him, has his baby, and then when he dies declares herself unable to go on living. In a perspicacious article, Ruth Solie describes this as a male fantasy, 'the *impersonation* of a woman by the voices of male culture'. And she pictures a typical nineteenth-century performance of these songs:

Though actually conveying the sentiments of men, they are of course to be performed by a woman, in a small and intimate room in someone's home, before people who are known to her and some of whom might well be potential suitors; she is unlikely to be a professional singer but, rather, someone's daughter or niece or cousin. . . . We are irresistibly reminded of the familiar cultural trope in which woman is positioned, docile and immobile, under the male gaze; and we are reminded, moreover, that it is a crucial part of the effectiveness of this fantasy that she appear to present *herself* so, to speak for herself.

This is performative meaning with a vengeance; the singer is not so much representing a patriarchal image of woman as enacting it, becoming it. (Indeed, if her future husband is in the audience, the performance will take on something of the character of a promise.) And in this way, singing *Frauenliebe* becomes as much a political act as singing 'Nkosi Sikelel' iAfrica'.

The role of a truly 'critical' musicology is, of course, to uncover this political content, to demonstrate the ideology implicated in what might otherwise appear as innocent and innocuous an act as the performance of a Schumann song cycle. But this will not be achieved by a pessimistic withdrawal from the music; on the contrary, it demands engagement with it—but an engagement that recognizes the music's worldliness and knowingly positions the interpreter in relation to it. And when I say 'interpreter', I do not exclude the sense in which that word is often used, namely to refer to the performer. After all, if a traditional performance of *Frauenliebe* identifies singer and protagonist, thereby constructing the singer/protagonist as the passive recipient of the male gaze, it must equally be possible to perform against the music, so to speak, and thus challenge this identification. At least, that is what k. d. lang does in her semi-staged performance of 'Johnnie Get Angry', in which the guilt-ridden protagonist asks her man to beat her; by subverting the relationship of protagonist and performer, lang succeeds in problematizing the sexual politics built into the song. In this way, the juxtaposition of Solie's and lang's interpretive practices suggests that the fullest engagement with music's gendered content will be achieved when we have not just feminist criticism of it, but feminist performance too.

Conclusion

In this book I have spoken of my cautious optimism about music: not just about music itself, but about our ability to understand it and use it as a means of personal and social transformation. As I see it, the way you become pessimistic is by assuming that music *represents* the world-views of cultures from which we are cut off by time, space, or both; divorced as we are from those cultures (the argument goes), we can't re-create the context within which the music might be intelligible, and so the more we think we understand it, the more we really don't. But this is reminiscent of the philosophical position known as solipsism, according to which the only way we can know the world is through our own subjective experience, from which it ultimately follows that you are a figment of my imagination (and I of yours), so that we all inhabit parallel, sealed-off universes. Once you accept that the only way you can know the world is through your own subjective experience, solipsism becomes the inevitable consequence; the way to avoid it is not to accept the premiss, but instead to regard human consciousness as something that is irreducibly public (or worldly, to borrow Lawrence Kramer's term again). Seen this way, the private experience on which solipsism is predicated is itself a social construction—an aspect, in fact, of the bourgeois subjectivity I have repeatedly spoken of. And my argument against musicological pessimism runs along similar lines.

If both music and musicology are ways of creating meaning rather than just of representing it, then we can see music as a means of gaining precisely the kind of insight into the cultural or historical other that a pessimistic musicology, like solipsism, proclaims to be impossible. In the previous chapter I described how music, and writing about music, can be seen as creating arenas for the negotiation of gender relations. But the principle is a much more general one; if music can communicate across barriers of gender difference, it can do so over other barriers as well. One example is music therapy, where music communicates across the cultural barrier of mental illness. But the most obvious example is the way we listen to the music of other cultures (or, perhaps even more significantly, the music of subcultures within our own broader culture). We do this not just for the good sounds, though there is that, but in order to gain some insight into those (sub)cultures. I have already quoted Philip Brett's description of music as 'an unmediated form of communication that is only by imperfect analogy called a language, "the" language of feeling'; it is this lack of overt mediation, the absence of mutually unintelligible vocabularies as in real languages, that leads people (not 'New' musicologists, to be sure) to describe music as a universal language.

And if we use music as a means of insight into other cultures, then equally we can see it as a means of negotiating cultural identity. We saw something of this in the case of 'Nkosi Sikelel' iAfrica'. But a more comprehensive example is postwar Australian music: composers like Peter Sculthorpe have brought together native Australian and East Asian influences in such a way as to contribute towards the broader cultural and political repositioning of Australia as an integral part of the emerging region of the Pacific Rim, rather than a

European culture on the wrong side of the world. A similar, though more conflicted, story might be told of the combination and separation of Chinese, other East Asian, and international styles of popular and 'art' music in postwar Hong Kong; music has given voice to the former colony's search for cultural identity, whether in its own right or, since 1997, as part of a larger entity. (It has not represented that search; it has been part of it.) If music did not enable some kind of cross-cultural communication then it could not be used this way. And this means that music becomes a way not only of gaining some understanding of the cultural other, but also of shifting your own position, constructing and reconstructing your own identity in the process. Music, in short, represents a way out of cultural pessimism.

And yet, the pessimists are right too (and remember, I spoke of *cautious* optimism). Woolly-minded optimism and modernist utopias pose their own perils. If music can be a means of cross-cultural understanding, it can be a means of cross-cultural misunderstanding, too; as Gary Tomlinson suggested, if we find the music of other times and places *too* easy to hear, too well adapted to our own modes of understanding and pleasure, then we are all too likely to assimilate it to our own values, to assume that we understand it in the same way that Western colonialists assumed they understood their subject peoples without ever seriously trying to find out what they had to say. Music may create the miraculous impression of going directly, as Beethoven wrote on the autograph of his *Missa Solemnis*, 'from the heart . . . to the heart!' But one person's miracle is another's illusion, and it is as true in a cultural as in a physical sense that there can be no music in a vacuum. To be sure, music can establish a point of connection between cultures. But it cannot abolish cultural difference at a stroke. At best it might be seen as a vantage point for becoming better aware of cultural difference; after all, differences stand out best against a background of similarity. Translated into terms of music, then, Bernard Shaw's dictum about Britain and America being separated by a common language might apply to the whole world.

'The essence of music as a cultural system', writes the ethnomusicologist Bruno Nettl, 'is both that it is *not* a . . . phenomenon of the natural world and also that *it is experienced as though it were.*' And that is why, as I see it, both the optimistic and the pessimistic positions are right (even though I think the former is more right, or more importantly right, than the latter). If we don't experience music as though it were a phenomenon of the natural world—as 'music', as people say—then we cut ourselves off from a means of understanding the other and overcoming difference, in however limited and provisional a manner; in a world in which we struggle for understanding we cannot afford to overlook what music has to offer, and this means active engagement with it, not a fastidious and melancholy withdrawal. But at the same time we need to know, and indeed to go on telling ourselves as we listen to it, that music is *not* a phenomenon of the natural world but a human construction. It is, *par excellence*, the artifice which disguises itself as nature. That is what makes it not only a source of sensory pleasure and an object of intellectual speculation, but also the ultimate hidden persuader.

And here we come back to the beginning of this book, to the masters of hidden persuasion in today's society, that is to say the advertisers. The music in the Prudential commercial which I discussed in the opening chapter speaks to each listener/viewer personally and confidentially, playing on unspoken values of authenticity and self-identity, whispering the message that, with Prudential, you can be what you want to be. As it does so, it effaces its own agency; you hear the advertiser's message, but you don't realize how much of it is coming from the music. In this way music naturalizes the message, makes it seem that—as I put it in Chapter 7—it is just 'the way things are'. No wonder, then, that so many stories warn against music's power to steal unawares into your mind and substitute its will for yours. Think of the Pied Piper of Hamlyn, whose playing lured the children away from their homes, never to be seen again; think of the ubiquitous stories of mermaids, or the sirens of ancient Greece, whose singing so entranced mariners that they were lured on to the rocks. Or think of the 'musical' voice of Saruman in Tolkien's *Lord of the Rings*, the model of the honey-tongued demagogue whose speech captivates his listeners even as they struggle to reject what he has to say.

That is why, in the end, it is not just musicologists who need to acquire a critical orientation. As Adorno clearly understood, critical theory omits music at its peril; music has unique powers as an agent of ideology. We need to understand its working, its charms, both to protect ourselves against them and, paradoxically, to enjoy them to the full. And in order to do that, we need to be able not just to hear music but to *read* it too: not in literal, notational terms, to be sure, but for its significance as an intrinsic part of culture, of society, of you and me.

References

Foreword

Elvis Costello compared writing about music with dancing about architecture in an interview, adding, 'It's a really stupid thing to want to do.' But it seems as if Thelonius Monk said it first; see Robert Walser, 'The Body in the Music: Epistemology and Musical Semiotics', *College Music Symposium*, 31 (1991), 117–26.

Chapter 1

I have written about the Prudential commercial ('Performance') at greater length in *Analysing Musical Multimedia* (Oxford: Clarendon Press, 1998). Details of the survival of emigré music in North America may be found in Philip Bohlman, 'Old World Cultures in North America', in Bruno Nettl *et al.*, *Excursions in World Music* (Englewood Cliffs, NJ: Prentice Hall, 1992), 278–324. For more details on the way in which heavy metal draws upon classical music, see Robert Walser, *Running with the Devil: Power, Gender, and Madness in Heavy Metal Music* (Hanover, NH: University Press of New England, 1993). A representative example of the 'new strain of critical writing' on rock to which I refer is Dave Headlam, 'Does the Song Remain the Same? Questions of Authorship and Identification in the Music of Led Zeppelin', in Elizabeth West Marvin and Richard Hermann (eds.), *Concert Music, Rock, and Jazz since 1945: Essays and Analytical Studies* (Rochester, NY: University of Rochester Press, 1995), 313–63. For a recently published, authoritative discussion of issues of value in popular music see Simon Frith, *Performing Rites: On the Value of Popular Music* (Oxford: Oxford University Press, 1996). Jean-Paul Sartre's remark about the concert hall burning down may be found in *Psychology of the Imagination* (London: Methuen, 1972), 224.

Chapter 2

On the Beethoven myth, with particular reference to the visual arts, see Alessandra Comini, *The Changing Image of Beethoven: A*

Study in Mythmaking (New York: Rizzoli, 1987); on the reception of Beethoven's music see Robin Wallace, *Beethoven's Critics: Aesthetic Dilemmas and Resolutions during the Composer's Lifetime* (Cambridge: Cambridge University Press, 1986). Details of the reception of the Ninth Symphony may be found in my *Beethoven: Symphony No. 9* (Cambridge: Cambridge University Press, 1993) or David Levy, *Beethoven: The Ninth Symphony* (New York: Schirmer, 1995). Maynard Solomon's *Beethoven*, the standard modern biography, is published by Schirmer (New York, 1977). Cambini's comments are quoted in Leo Schrade, *Beethoven in France: The Growth of an Idea* (New Haven: Yale University Press, 1942), 3. Beethoven wrote that 'the best of us obtain joy through suffering' in his letter of 19 October 1815 to Countess Erdödy (*The Letters of Beethoven*, ed. and trans. Emily Anderson (London: Macmillan, 1961), no. 63). For the ambivalent status of the 'Ode to Joy' within the EU see Caryl Clark, 'Forging Identity: Beethoven's "Ode" as European Anthem', *Critical Inquiry*, 23 (1997), 789–807. I have drawn the term 'the imaginary museum of musical works' from the title of Lydia Goehr's book *The Imaginary Museum of Musical Works: An Essay in the Philosophy of Music* (Oxford: Clarendon Press, 1992). The quotations from Schenker may be found in 'Mozart: Symphony in G minor', in Heinrich Schenker, *The Masterwork in Music: A Yearbook, Vol. 2 (1926)*, ed. William Drabkin (Cambridge: Cambridge University Press, 1996), 59–96 (p. 60), *Harmony*, ed. Oswald Jonas, trans. Elisabeth Mann Borgese (Chicago: Chicago University Press, 1954), 69, 60, and *Free Composition* (New York: Longman, 1979), i. 160. Scott Burnham's comment on music and words is taken from his chapter 'How Music Matters: Poetic Content Revisited', in Nicholas Cook and Mark Everist (eds.), *Rethinking Music* (Oxford: Oxford University Press, 1998), 193–216.

Chapter 3

Birtwistle's remark about audiences was quoted in the 'They Said It' column, *The Daily Telegraph*, Saturday, 30 March 1996, Arts section, 3. ROCK AROUND THE WORLD (RATW) is a Los Angeles-based internet site developed from the 1970s syndicated radio interview show of the same name, containing audio samples of new releases as well as reviews, photographs, and an archive of historic materials; its URL is http://www.ratw.com. (As I write, the web is rapidly becoming the way to find out about new music; high-profile works like Paul McCartney's *Standing Stone* have their own web sites, with recordings, videos, and interviews to download.) A representative example of the kind of appreciation/history textbook I refer to is Joseph Kerman (with Vivian Kerman), *Listen*, 3rd edn. (New York: Worth Publishers, Inc., 1980). A convenient introduction to Schoenberg in general, and the Society for Private Performances in particular, is Charles Rosen, *Schoenberg* (London: Fontana, 1976). Peter Sellars's description of the condition of classical music, originally published in the *Los Angeles Times* (26 Dec. 1996) is quoted in Philip Brett, 'Round Table VIII: Cultural Politics', *Acta Musicologica*, 59 (1997), 48. The quotation by Lawrence Kramer comes from his book *Classical Music and Postmodern Knowledge* (Berkeley and Los Angeles: University of California Press, 1995), 3–4.

Chapter 4

I have discussed many of the matters contained in this chapter in *Music, Imagination, and Culture* (Oxford: Clarendon Press, 1990), where a transcription of Fig. 14 may be found (p. 221). Alessandro Moreschi's recording of Gounod's *Ave Maria* is available on 'Moreschi—The Last Castrato', Pearl Opal CD 9823. For a brief introduction to *qin* music and notation, see (David) Liang Mingyue, *Music of the Billion: An Introduction to Chinese Musical Culture* (New York: Heinrichshofen Edition, 1985). The translation of the letter attributed to Mozart (first published in the *Allgemeine musikalische Zeitung*) is taken from J. R. Schultz (trans.), 'An Unpublished Letter of Mozart', *Harmonicon*, 3 (1825), 198–200. Schlösser's account of the meeting with Beethoven is translated in Elliot Forbes (ed.), *Thayer's Life of Beethoven* (Princeton: Princeton University Press, 1964), 851. For the authoritative discussion of the authenticity of these two sources, see Maynard Solomon, 'Beethoven's Creative Process: A Two-Part Invention', in Solomon, *Beethoven Essays* (Cambridge, Mass.: Harvard University Press, 1988), 126–38. For the link with theological conceptions of creation, see Peter Kivy, 'Mozart and Monotheism', in *The Fine Art of Repetition: Essays in the Philosophy of Music* (Cambridge: Cambridge University Press,

1993), 189–99. The quotation from Gustav Nottebohm is taken from *Two Beethoven Sketchbooks: A Description With Musical Extracts* (London: Gollancz, 1979), 98; originally published 1880. Ligeti's description of *San Francisco Polyphony* appeared on the Grammofonfirma BIS recording of that and other works by Ligeti (BIS LP-53, c.1976). On musical movement, and more generally on embedded metaphor in music, see Roger Scruton, *The Aesthetics of Music* (Oxford: Oxford University Press, 1997). Richard Dawkins explains his idea of the 'river of genes' in *River out of Eden: A Darwinian View of Life* (London: Phoenix, 1995).

Chapter 5

Joanna Hodge's account of the 'constructivist' view of art, which includes references to Wittgenstein's writings, is published as 'Aesthetic Decomposition: Music, Identity, and Time', in Michael Krausz (ed.), *The Interpretation of Music: Philosophical Essays* (Oxford: Clarendon Press, 1993), 247–58. The idea that music presages social development has been put forward by Jacques Attali, *Noise: The Political Economy of Music* (Manchester: Manchester University Press, 1985). Schoenberg's comments on performers are quoted in Dika Newlin, *Schoenberg Remembered: Diaries and Recollections (1938–76)* (New York: Pendragon, 1980), 164.

Chapter 6

Kerman's book was published as *Contemplating Music* (Cambridge, Mass.: Harvard University Press, 1985) and *Musicology* (London: Fontana, 1985); his article 'How We Got into Analysis, and How to Get Out' appeared in *Critical Inquiry*, 7 (1980), 311–31. Jonathan Del Mar's edition of Beethoven's Ninth Symphony is published by Bärenreiter (BA 9009); first recorded by The Hanover Band (conductor Roy Goodman) on Nimbus NI5134. For the 'authenticity' debate, see Nicholas Kenyon (ed.), *Authenticity and Early Music: A Symposium* (Oxford: Oxford University Press, 1988), in particular Richard Taruskin's contribution ('The Pastness of the Present and the Presence of the Past', pp. 137–210). Kay Kaufman Shelemay gives an account of her work with the Beta Israel community in *A Song of Longing: An Ethiopian Journey* (Urbana, Ill.: University of Illinois Press,

1991). In the penultimate sentence I am making an oblique reference to Philip Bohlman, 'Musicology as a Political Act', *Journal of Musicology*, 11 (1993), 411–36.

Chapter 7

For an introduction to Adorno's thinking about music, and his extensive publications, see Max Paddison, *Adorno's Aesthetics of Music* (Cambridge: Cambridge University Press, 1993). The College Music Society report is *Music in the Undergraduate Curriculum: A Reassessment* (Boulder, Colo.: The College Music Society, Inc., 1989); it deals specifically with the curriculum for non-majors in Music (i.e. students taking it as only a subsidiary element of their course). For reviews of Cécile Chaminade, as well as a balanced account of gender issues in music generally, see Marcia J. Citron, *Gender and the Musical Canon* (Cambridge: Cambridge University Press, 1993); the passages I quote from Vincent d'Indy's *Cours de composition musicale* may be found on p. 136. Other sources to which I refer are, in alphabetical order by author, Philip Brett, 'Musicality, Essentialism, and the Closet', in Philip Brett, Elizabeth Wood, and Gary C. Thomas (eds.), *Queering the Pitch: The New Gay and Lesbian Musicology* (New York: Routledge, 1994), 9–26; Suzanne Cusick, 'On a Lesbian Relationship with Music: A Serious Effort Not to Think Straight', in Brett *et al.* (eds.), *Queering the Pitch*, 67–83; Susan McClary, *Feminine Endings: Music, Gender, and Sexuality* (Minneapolis: Minnesota University Press, 1991) and 'Constructions of Subjectivity in Schubert's Music', in Brett *et al.* (eds.), *Queering the Pitch*, 205–33; Martha Mockus, 'Queer Thoughts on Country Music and k. d. lang', in Brett *et al.* (eds.), *Queering the Pitch*, 257–71; Maynard Solomon, 'Franz Schubert and the Peacocks of Benvenuto Cellini', *19th-Century Music*, 12 (1989), 193–206; Pieter van den Toorn, *Music, Politics, and the Academy* (Berkeley and Los Angeles: University of California Press, 1995), 37; James Webster, 'Music, Pathology, Sexuality, Beethoven, Schubert', *19th-Century Music*, 17 (1994), 89–93 (this number of *19th-Century Music*— vol. 17, no. 1—was exclusively devoted to the issue of Schubert's homosexuality). The exchange between Lawrence Kramer and Gary Tomlinson began in 1992 with Kramer's article 'The Musicology of the Future', published in the inaugural issue of the journal *repercussions* and subsequently incorporated into chapter 1 of his *Classical Music and Postmodern Knowledge*, and continued in *Current Musicology*, 53 (1993), 18–40. Ruth Solie's reading of *Frauenliebe* is published as 'Whose Life? The Gendered Self in Schumann's *Frauenliebe* Songs', in Stephen Paul Scher (ed.), *Music and Text: Critical Inquiries* (Cambridge: Cambridge University Press, 1992), 219–40. k. d. lang's performance of 'Johnnie Get Angry' is available on the video 'k. d. lang: Harvest of Seven Years (Cropped and Chronicled)', Warner 7599 38234-3 (PAL), 38234 (NTSC); for a commentary, see Lori Burns, ' "Joanie" Get Angry: k. d. lang's Feminist Revision', in John Covach and Graeme Boone (eds.), *Analyzing Rock Music* (New York: Oxford University Press, 1997), 93–112. Finally, the quotation from Ludwig Tieck is taken from Susan McClary, 'Narrative Agendas in "Absolute" Music', in Ruth Solie (ed.), *Musicology and Difference: Gender and Sexuality in Music Scholarship* (Berkeley and Los Angeles: University of California Press, 1993), 326–44, while Karajan's comment is quoted in Sally Morris and Katie Price, 'Calling the Tune', *Spare Rib* (Nov. 1986); my thanks to Sophie Fuller for this reference.

Conclusion

The quotation from Bruno Nettl is taken from his *Heartland Excursions: Ethnomusicological Reflections on Schools of Music* (Urbana, Ill.: Illinois University Press, 1995), 181.

Index

Page numbers in italic refer to figures

OXFORD

MORE OXFORD PAPERBACKS

This book is just one of nearly 1000 Oxford Paperbacks currently in print. If you would like details of other Oxford Paperbacks, including titles in the World's Classics, Oxford Reference, Oxford Books, OPUS, Past Masters, Oxford Authors, and Oxford Shakespeare series, please write to:

UK and Europe: Oxford Paperbacks Publicity Manager, Arts and Reference Publicity Department, Oxford University Press, Walton Street, Oxford OX2 6DP.

Customers in UK and Europe will find Oxford Paperbacks available in all good bookshops. But in case of difficulty please send orders to the Cash-with-Order Department, Oxford University Press Distribution Services, Saxon Way West, Corby, Northants NN18 9ES. Tel: 01536 741519; Fax: 01536 746337. Please send a cheque for the total cost of the books, plus £1.75 postage and packing for orders under £20; £2.75 for orders over £20. Customers outside the UK should add 10% of the cost of the books for postage and packing.

USA: Oxford Paperbacks Marketing Manager, Oxford University Press, Inc., 200 Madison Avenue, New York, N.Y. 10016.

Canada: Trade Department, Oxford University Press, 70 Wynford Drive, Don Mills, Ontario M3C 1J9.

Australia: Trade Marketing Manager, Oxford University Press, G.P.O. Box 2784Y, Melbourne 3001, Victoria.

South Africa: Oxford University Press, P.O. Box 1141, Cape Town 8000.

CLASSICS

Mary Beard and John Henderson

This *Very Short Introduction* to Classics links a haunting temple on a lonely mountainside to the glory of ancient Greece and the grandeur of Rome, and to Classics within modern culture—from Jefferson and Byron to Asterix and Ben-Hur.

'This little book should be in the hands of every student, and every tourist to the lands of the ancient world . . . a splendid piece of work'
Peter Wiseman
Author of *Talking to Virgil*

'an eminently readable and useful guide to many of the modern debates enlivening the field . . . the most up-to-date and accessible introduction available'
Edith Hall
Author of *Inventing the Barbarian*

'lively and up-to-date . . . it shows classics as a living enterprise, not a warehouse of relics'
New Statesman and Society

'nobody could fail to be informed and entertained—the accent of the book is provocative and stimulating'
Times Literary Supplement

ARCHAEOLOGY

Paul Bahn

'Archaeology starts, really, at the point when the first recognizable 'artefacts' appear—on current evidence, that was in East Africa about 2.5 million years ago—and stretches right up to the present day. What you threw in the garbage yesterday, no matter how useless, disgusting, or potentially embarrassing, has now become part of the recent archaeological record.'

This Very Short Introduction reflects the enduring popularity of archaeology—a subject which appeals as a pastime, career, and academic discipline, encompasses the whole globe, and surveys 2.5 million years. From deserts to jungles, from deep caves to mountain-tops, from pebble tools to satellite photographs, from excavation to abstract theory, archaeology interacts with nearly every other discipline in its attempts to reconstruct the past.

'very lively indeed and remarkably perceptive . . . a quite brilliant and level-headed look at the curious world of archaeology'
Professor Barry Cunliffe,
University of Oxford

BUDDHISM

Damien Keown

'Karma can be either good or bad. Buddhists speak of good karma as "merit", and much effort is expended in acquiring it. Some picture it as a kind of spiritual capital—like money in a bank account—whereby credit is built up as the deposit on a heavenly rebirth.'

This Very Short Introduction introduces the reader both to the teachings of the Buddha and to the integration of Buddhism into daily life. What are the distinctive features of Buddhism? Who was the Buddha, and what are his teachings? How has Buddhist thought developed over the centuries, and how can contemporary dilemmas be faced from a Buddhist perspective?

'Damien Keown's book is a readable and wonderfully lucid introduction to one of mankind's most beautiful, profound, and compelling systems of wisdom. The rise of the East makes understanding and learning from Buddhism, a living doctrine, more urgent than ever before. Keown's impressive powers of explanation help us to come to terms with a vital contemporary reality.'
Bryan Appleyard